MAXIMIZE YOUR WRITING

2

Maximize Your Writing 2

Pearson Education, Inc., 221 River Street, Hoboken, NJ 07030 USA

Staff credits: The people who made up the *Maximize Your Writing* team are Pietro Alongi, Rhea Banker, Tracey Munz Cataldo, Mindy DePalma, Gina DiLillo, Niki Lee, Amy McCormick, Lindsay Richman, and Paula Van Ells.

Text composition: MPS North America LLC
Design: EMC Design Ltd
Photo credit: Cover, PHOTOCREO Michal Bednarek / Shutterstock

ISBN-13: 978-0-13-466142-1   ISBN-10: 0-13-466142-7

Printed in the United States of America
2   16

pearsonelt.com/maximizeyourwriting

CONTENTS

Pre-Test 1

In the timed Pre-Test 1, you will demonstrate how well you understand sentence structure, grammar, punctuation, mechanics, and organization. You have 50 minutes to complete the test. To mark your answer, circle the letter of the correct choice.

1 Rafael is _____ his brother.

    a funnier than

    b more funny than

    c more funnier than

    d funnier

2 Martina _____ .

    a finished her work fastly

    b finished her work fast

    c finished fast her work

    d finished fastly her work

3 Sofia _____ to work.

    a takes often the train

    b often takes the train

    c often the train takes

    d the train often takes

4 On your way home from work, please buy _____ .

    a some milks

    b a milk

    c two milks

    d some milk

5 If you don't hurry, you _____ the bus.

    a miss

    b missing

    c will miss

    d are missing

6 Nina doesn't know if she _____ to the party.

    a can go

    b can to go

    c can going

    d cans go

7 You _____ the teacher to repeat the instructions.

    a should to ask

    b should asking

    c should ask

    d should asks

8 Zara _____ with friends than alone.

    a would rather study

    b would rather to study

    c rather would study

    d rather would studies

9 What is _____ that box?

    a between

    b on the right

    c inside

    d on top

10 Please put the newspaper _____ the table.

    a in

    b on

    c at

    d from

11 Yoshi _____ more than five hours of television every day.

    a is watch

    b watching

    c watches

    d watch

12 Don't call John now. He _____ .

    a sleeps

    b sleep

    c sleeping

    d is sleeping

13 Cristina _____ to school yesterday.

    a not go

    b didn't go

    c didn't going

    d not did go

14 I was in Buenos Aires last _____ .

    a january

    b Winter

    c thanksgiving

    d November

15 Since _____ Adina has very few friends.

    a , she is shy

    b she is shy,

    c she is shy

    d , she is shy.

16 Anh has a car _____ he doesn't drive very often.

    a , but

    b but,

    c but

    d , but,

17 Shira washed the kitchen floor _____ she cleaned the bathroom.

    a . After that,

    b , after that

    c After that

    d , after that,

18 Rani has many hobbies _____ he enjoys dancing, reading, and playing cards.

    a , for example

    b , for example,

    c for example

    d . For example,

19 "I'm going to be a doctor like my mother _____ the boy said.

    a ,

    b ,"

    c ",

    d ."

20 Jacinta was born on _____ .

    a April 14 1998

    b April 14, 1998

    c April, 14, 1998

    d April-14-1998

21 Would you like coffee _____ tea?

    a , or

    b or you prefer

    c or, do you prefer

    d , or do you prefer

22 I lost my phone, _____ I couldn't call you.

    a and

    b or

    c but

    d so

23 _____ he got married, Chao lived with his parents.

  a Before

  b After that

  c As soon

  d While

24 Yolanda decided to be an engineer _____ she's good at math.

  a since

  b for

  c if

  d when

25 I phoned my parents _____ .

  a , as soon as my plane landed

  b as soon as my plane landed

  c , my plane landed

  d my plane landed

26 I want a car _____ doesn't use a lot of gas.

  a who

  b that

  c which

  d whom

27 The instructions for using my new phone _____ confusing.

  a are

  b is

  c be

  d was

28 Which item is a complete sentence?

  a My grandmother, who graduated from Harvard University.

  b If you want to learn more about dinosaurs.

  c A sari is the traditional dress of women in South Asia.

  d The book you want on the table.

29 Which item is written incorrectly?

  a Some students live in the dormitory others live in apartments.

  b Some students live in the dormitory, and others live in apartments.

  c Some students live in the dormitory. Others live in apartments.

  d Some students live in the dormitory. In contrast, others live in apartments.

30 Which item is written incorrectly?

  a Paul wants to be a teacher. He likes working with children.

  b Paul wants to be a teacher, he likes working with children.

  c Paul wants to be a teacher because he likes working with children.

  d Paul likes working with children, so he wants to be a teacher.

31 This is how my teacher, Mrs. Brand, prepares her lesson plans. To begin, she sits at her desk and organizes her papers and books. _____ , she decides that she needs a cup of coffee. She goes to the kitchen, boils water, and prepares her drink.

   a After

   b Next

   c As soon as

   d Third

32 If you want to succeed in school, there are several things you can do. First, complete all your assignments. If you're having trouble, don't be afraid to ask for help. Second, take good notes. Be sure to write down all the main points your teacher makes. Next, attend all your classes, and sit in the front row so that you can hear your teacher clearly. _____ , don't wait until the last day to study for an exam. Start early so that you have plenty of time.

   a As a result

   b Most importantly

   c Final

   d Before

33 Five U.S. states border the Gulf of Mexico. Starting in the east, the first state is Florida. Moving west, the next state is Alabama. Mississippi is _____ of the five states. Louisiana is west of Mississippi, and Texas is west of Louisiana.

   a across

   b in front

   c between

   d in the middle

34 The ice that covers the North Pole and Antarctica is melting quickly _____ higher temperatures on Earth. For example, the thickness of Arctic ice has decreased by 40 percent since 1960.

   a since

   b because of

   c when

   d then

35 The weak economic situation has hurt my hometown in several ways. First, many local businesses failed. _____ , many workers lost their jobs.

   a Because

   b Due to

   c Since

   d As a result

36 In some ways, the government of India is _____ the government of the United States. Both countries have a president.

   a alike

   b also

   c similar to

   d the same

37 The length of American women's skirts changes every few years. For example, during the 1940s and 1950s, knee-length skirts were in fashion. _____ , very short skirts were the style in the 1960s.

   a Different

   b But

   c Unlike

   d On the other hand

38 _____ , every young person should spend one year doing volunteer work after high school. I have several reasons for this idea. First, volunteering teaches young people to be responsible.

   a In my view

   b However

   c I am against

   d As a result

39 The San Diego Zoo is home to many rare and endangered animals. _____ , you can see a giant panda there.

   a Such as

   b For instance

   c One

   d Because

40 Read the topic sentence. Which words are the controlling idea (tell what specific details the paragraph will discuss)?

Topic sentence: These days, high-fructose corn syrup is used to sweeten soft drinks, juices, and candies.

   a These days

   b high-fructose corn syrup

   c is used

   d is used to sweeten soft drinks, juices, and candies

Pre-Test 2

In the timed Pre-Test 2, you will demonstrate how well you can write about a topic. Pay attention to sentence structure, grammar, punctuation, mechanics, organization, and vocabulary.

Write about the following topic or the topic your teacher assigns. You have 50 minutes to complete the test.

Write a paragraph describing a holiday from your country. When is it? What is the holiday about? What do people eat, do, and wear?

_____

_____

_____

_____

_____

_____

_____

_____

_____

_____

_____

_____

_____

_____

_____

_____

_____

_____

_____

_____

PUNCTUATION AND MECHANICS

Capital Letters

PROPER NOUNS AND PRONOUNS

Presentation

Capital Letters: Proper Nouns and Pronouns

Capitalize the following words in English:

Categories		
The first word of a sentence	Names of places, including streets, cities, states, countries, lakes, seas, deserts, and areas of the world	Days of the week and month (but not seasons)
The pronoun *I*		Names of school courses with numbers
Names of people	Names of languages, religions, and nationalities	Names of specific businesses and schools
Holidays		

Practice 1

Circle the words that are capitalized correctly.

Example:

1 *the(The) concert is on friday.(Friday) night.*

2 Last summer/Summer, my family took an unforgettable trip to thailand/Thailand.

3 where/Where is the nearest post office/Post Office?

4 I visited my cousin/Cousin, who is a student at yale university/Yale University.

5 Sofia speaks french/French but not spanish/Spanish.

6 There's a gas station/Gas Station on pico boulevard/Pico Boulevard.

7 Are you going to toronto/Toronto for thanksgiving/Thanksgiving?

8 Mitra is enrolled in chemistry/Chemistry 102.

9 In Europe, there are christians/Christians, jews/Jews, and muslims/Muslims.

10 I love italian/Italian food, especially pizza/Pizza.

11 The second semester/Semester will begin in january/January.

Practice 2

Underline the words that require capital letters.

1 In the summer, there are concerts in the park every friday evening.

2 traditional thanksgiving foods include turkey with stuffing, sweet potatoes, and pumpkin pie for dessert.

3 robert is a student at washington university. his major is psychology. this semester he is taking psychology 102.

4 when she was in high school, yasmine worked at funland during summers and christmas vacations.

5 my husband and i have traveled all over the middle east.

6 cara has a doctor's appointment next wednesday at 2 p.m.

7 be careful when you drive down adams avenue.

8 kelly works for proprintco in seattle.

ACRONYMS AND PERSONAL TITLES

Practice 1

Read each sentence. Circle the letter of the correct form.

Example:

1 *My neighbor's name is _____ Saxon.*
   a *mrs.*
   (b) *Mrs.*

2 I have an appointment with _____ Wat on Thursday.
   a dr.
   b Dr.

3 Our neighbor, _____ Jones, allows us to swim in his pool.
   a mr.
   b Mr.

4 Who is your economics _____ ?
   a professor
   b Professor

5 We listened to the _____ speech.
  a prime minister's
  b Prime Minister's

6 Thousands of people waited in the rain to see the _____ .
  a queen
  b Queen

7 The _____ lives in Vatican City.
  a pope
  b Pope

8 Please address your letter to _____ Kim.
  a manager
  b Manager

9 The students visited the White House and met _____ Obama.
  a president
  b President

10 Tonight I'm having dinner with my _____ .
  a uncle
  b Uncle

11 My favorite teacher is _____ Adams.
  a professor
  b Professor

Practice 2

Rewrite the underlined phrase as an abbreviation.

Example:

1 *Her car is a Volkswagen.* _____VW_____

2 She's studying at the University of Michigan. _____

3 Thousand of tourists visit the United Nations every year. _____

4 My sister lives in the United Kingdom. _____

5 Karen has a Bachelor of Arts in French. _____

6 We enjoyed our visit to Washington, District of Columbia. _____

7 Please send me your answer as soon as possible. _____

8 There's an automatic teller machine at the supermarket. _____

9 I wanted to use my debit card, but I couldn't remember my personal identification number. _____

10 The number of people with human immunodeficiency virus has gone down dramatically. _____

11 I have cousins in the People's Republic of China. _____

Commas

COMMAS IN COMPLEX SENTENCES WITH DEPENDENT CLAUSES

> **Presentation**
>
> **Commas in Complex Sentences with Dependent Clauses**
>
> Complex sentences have one independent clause and one or more dependent clauses. Dependent clauses begin with words called subordinators. Common subordinators include:
>
> **Time:** before, after, as soon as, since, when, while
>
> **Reason:** because, since
>
> **Condition:** if
>
> Follow these rules for punctuating complex sentences:
>
> | Rules | Examples |
> | --- | --- |
> | If you write the dependent clause first, then put a comma after it. | **When Adam was eight years old,** he got a tuba. |
> | If you write the independent clause first, then don't use a comma. | **Adam got a tuba** when he was eight years old. |

Practice 1

Read the sentence. Is the comma used correctly? Circle the letter of your answer.

Example:

1 *I admire my father, because he is hardworking and honest.*
  a *Correct*
  (b) *Incorrect*

2 When it began to rain Kelly closed the windows.
  a Correct
  b Incorrect

3 Because he gets nervous on airplanes, Edmond doesn't like to fly.
  a Correct
  b Incorrect

4 Since Monday is a holiday, we don't have to work.
  a Correct
  b Incorrect

5 I'll go to the supermarket, as soon as it stops raining.

   a Correct
   b Incorrect

6 If the world's population continues to grow there will not be enough food to feed everybody.

   a Correct
   b Incorrect

7 Robert has to cancel his European vacation because he forgot to renew his passport.

   a Correct
   b Incorrect

8 We learned a few Turkish phrases before we visited Istanbul last year.

   a Correct
   b Incorrect

9 I have more energy, if I exercise every day.

   a Correct
   b Incorrect

10 Please don't use a cell phone while you're in the library.

   a Correct
   b Incorrect

11 We're going to get caught in rush-hour traffic, if we don't leave the house right now.

   a Correct
   b Incorrect

Practice 2

Circle the letter of the sentence in each set that has correct punctuation.

1 a Please clean up your room before you go out to play.
   b Please clean up your room, before you go out to play.
   c Please clean up your room before, you go out to play.

2 a The Mata family moved to Chicago, because Mr. Mata got a job there.
   b The Mata family moved to Chicago because Mr. Mata got a job there.
   c The Mata family moved to Chicago because, Mr. Mata got a job there.

3 a Be sure to lock the door, when you leave.
   b Be sure to lock the door when, you leave.
   c Be sure to lock the door when you leave.

4 a Since my father is a vegetarian, our family seldom eats meat.
   b Since my father is a vegetarian our family seldom eats meat.
   c Since, my father is a vegetarian our family seldom eats meat.

5 a I felt very sad after, the movie ended.
   b I felt very sad, after the movie ended.
   c I felt very sad after the movie ended.

6 a If you can wait half an hour I'll give you a ride home.
   b If you can wait half an hour, I'll give you a ride home.
   c If you can, wait half an hour I'll give you a ride home.

7 a Peter sold his motorcycle after, he was in a serious accident.

   b Peter sold his motorcycle, after he was in a serious accident.

   c Peter sold his motorcycle after he was in a serious accident.

8 a While Jennifer waited for the train, she checked the messages on her phone.

   b While Jennifer waited for the train she checked the messages on her phone.

   c While, Jennifer waited for the train she checked the messages, on her phone.

9 a If you don't wear a hat you're going to get sunburned.

   b If you don't wear a hat, you're going to get sunburned.

   c If, you don't wear a hat, you're going to get sunburned.

10 a Ali never saw snow, before he came to study in Wisconsin.

   b Ali never saw snow before he came to study in Wisconsin.

   c Ali never saw snow, before, he came to study in Wisconsin.

11 a It's polite to say "Excuse me" if you step on someone's foot.

   b It's polite, to say "Excuse me" if you step on someone's foot.

   c It's polite to say "Excuse me," if you step on someone's foot.

COMMAS IN COMPOUND SENTENCES WITH COORDINATING CONJUNCTIONS

Presentation

Commas in Compound Sentences with Coordinating Conjunctions

A *compound sentence* consists of two simple sentences and a connecting word called a coordinating conjunction (*and, or, but, so*). Compound sentences normally have a comma.

Follow these rules to punctuate compound sentences correctly.

Rules	Examples
Put a comma before the conjunction in compound sentences.	I have an iPod, **and** I listen to it every day.
	I have a digital camera, **but** I don't use it much
Do not use a comma in sentences that have a compound verb.	Carolyn **lives** in Poland **and speaks** Polish.
It is not necessary to use a comma in compound sentences that are very short.	Turn left and go two blocks.

Practice 1

Read each sentence. Look at punctuation. Are commas used or omitted in the right places? Circle the letter of your answer.

Example:

1 *Pablo sings, and plays guitar in a rock band.*
   a *Correct*
   ⓑ *Incorrect*

2 Josie lives and works in Manhattan.
   a Correct
   b Incorrect

3 Her office is downtown so she can walk to work most of the time.
   a Correct
   b Incorrect

4 Shopping is very convenient, and there are many excellent restaurants nearby.
   a Correct
   b Incorrect

5 On weekends, she often goes to museums or attends lectures.
  a Correct
  b Incorrect

6 However, she doesn't like running through traffic, or tolerating noise in the big city.
  a Correct
  b Incorrect

7 Her apartment is tiny and the rent is high.
  a Correct
  b Incorrect

8 Her family lives far away so she feels lonely sometimes.
  a Correct
  b Incorrect

9 Manhattan is full of people but it's not easy to make friends.
  a Correct
  b Incorrect

10 Now she is single, so she thinks the advantages of living downtown are greater than the disadvantages.
  a Correct
  b Incorrect

11 Someday she hopes to buy a house in the suburbs, and plant a garden.
  a Correct
  b Incorrect

Practice 2

Circle the letter of the sentence in each set that has the correct punctuation.

1 a Rodolfo works at home so he doesn't need to wear a suit.
  b Rodolfo works at home so, he doesn't need to wear a suit.
  c Rodolfo works at home, so he doesn't need to wear a suit.

2 a Riding a bicycle is fun and it's good for my health.
  b Riding a bicycle is fun, and it's good for my health.
  c Riding a bicycle is fun and, it's good for my health.

3 a Bicycles don't use gas, so they don't pollute the environment.
  b Bicycles don't use gas so they don't pollute the environment.
  c Bicycles don't use gas so, they don't pollute the environment.

4 a A bicycle can cost $80 or, it can cost $800.
  b A bicycle can cost $80 or it can cost $800.
  c A bicycle can cost $80, or it can cost $800.

5 a Bicycles are cheaper than cars, and you don't need to buy insurance.
  b Bicycles are cheaper than cars and you don't need to buy insurance.
  c Bicycles are cheaper than cars and, you don't need to buy insurance.

6 a I have a car but, I rarely use it.
  b I have a car, but I rarely use it.
  c I have a car but I rarely, use it.

7 **a** Riding a bicycle is fun but it can be dangerous.

   b Riding a bicycle is fun, but it can be dangerous.

   c Riding a bicycle is fun but it can be dangerous.

8 **a** Cars go fast and, bikes are hard to see.

   b Cars go fast and bikes, are hard to see.

   c Cars go fast, and bikes are hard to see.

9 **a** My friend was hit by a car last year but, he wasn't badly injured.

   b My friend was hit by a car last year but he wasn't badly injured.

   c My friend was hit by a car last year, but he wasn't badly injured.

10 **a** Some drivers get angry at cyclists and shout at them.

   b Some drivers get angry at cyclists, and shout at them.

   c Some drivers get angry at cyclists and, shout at them.

11 **a** Get a bike and have fun!

   b Get a bike, and have fun!

   c Get a bike and, have fun!

COMMAS FOR ITEMS IN A SERIES

> **Presentation**
>
> **Commas for Items in a Series**
>
> A series is a group of three or more nouns, verbs, or adjectives.
>
> Follow these rules for using commas with items in a series.
>
> | Rules | Examples |
> |---|---|
> | Use a comma after each item in a series of three or more. | There are students in my English class from Japan, China, Sweden, Qatar, and Mexico. |
> | Do not use a comma between two items connected with a conjunction. | Would you like coffee or tea? |

Practice 1

Read each sentence. Look at punctuation. Are commas used correctly or incorrectly? Circle the letter of the correct answer.

Example:

1 *I made an omelette of eggs, spinach, cheese, chili, and mushrooms.*
   a *Correct*
   b *Incorrect*

2 Barbara enjoys taking pictures of dogs, cats and birds.
   a Correct
   b Incorrect

3 You can get to the beach by bus, by car, or by bicycle.
   a Correct
   b Incorrect

4 Susanna's hair is long black and shiny.
   a Correct
   b Incorrect

5 I always travel with a laptop computer and a cell phone.
   a Correct
   b Incorrect

6 Jane's computer, cell phone, wallet sunglasses and hat were stolen from her car.
   a Correct
   b Incorrect

7 There are fruit trees in the front yard, and in the back yard.
   a Correct
   b Incorrect

8 Why don't you come in, sit down, and have a cold drink?
   a Correct
   b Incorrect

9 On our vacation we plan to swim sail hike and ride bikes.
   a Correct
   b Incorrect

10 Female gymnasts are tiny but very strong.

   a Correct

   b Incorrect

11 The apartment comes with a washing machine, a dryer a dishwasher a stove, and a refrigerator.

   a Correct

   b Incorrect

Practice 2

Read the set of sentences. Circle the letter of the sentence that uses correct punctuation.

Example:

1 a *I made a salad of lettuce tomatoes cucumber bell pepper, and mushrooms.*

   b *I made a salad of lettuce, tomatoes, cucumber bell pepper and mushrooms.*

   c *I made a salad of lettuce, tomatoes, cucumber, bell pepper, and mushrooms.*

2 a In the next five years, Brad plans to finish college get a job and get married.

   b In the next five years, Brad plans to finish college, get a job, and get married.

   c In the next five years, Brad plans to finish college, get a job and get married.

3 a Next week, I have tests in history psychology Italian and physics.

   b Next week, I have tests in history psychology, Italian and physics.

   c Next week, I have tests in history, psychology, Italian, and physics.

4 a There were dog toys on the kitchen floor, under the sofa, on the dining room table, and in the bathtub.

   b There were dog toys on the kitchen floor under the sofa on the dining room table, and in the bathtub.

   c There were dog toys on the kitchen floor under the sofa on the dining room table and in the bathtub.

5 a Mr. Collins will travel to New York Pennsylvania New Jersey and Connecticut.

   b Mr. Collins will travel to New York, Pennsylvania, New Jersey, and Connecticut.

   c Mr. Collins will travel to New York Pennsylvania New Jersey, and Connecticut.

6 a Dinner consisted of soup chicken, salad, rice and fruit.

   b Dinner consisted of soup chicken salad, rice and fruit.

   c Dinner consisted of soup, chicken, salad, rice, and fruit.

7 a Marc, Melanie, Josie, and Jerry worked on the project together.

   b Marc Melanie Josie and Jerry worked on the project together.

   c Marc, Melanie, Josie and Jerry worked on the project together.

8 a Our tour of the campus included the dorms science labs cafeteria and gym.

   b Our tour of the campus included the dorms science labs cafeteria, and gym.

   c Our tour of the campus included the dorms, science labs, cafeteria, and gym.

9 a The hotel room is large bright well-furnished, and comfortable.

   b The hotel room is large, bright, well-furnished, and comfortable.

   c The hotel room is large bright, well-furnished and comfortable.

10 a The events in a triathlon include swimming running and bicycling.

   b The events in a triathlon include swimming running, and bicycling.

   c The events in a triathlon include swimming, running, and bicycling.

11 a Most of the women at the wedding wore long gowns, high heels, and expensive jewelry.

   b Most of the women at the wedding wore long gowns high heels and expensive jewelry.

   c Most of the women at the wedding wore long gowns high heels, and expensive jewelry.

COMMAS WITH TIME AND ORDER SIGNALS

Presentation

Commas with Time and Order Signals

Use time and order signals to show a sequence of events or steps in a process. Common time and order signals include:

Signal Words: first, first of all, second (third, fourth, etc.), next, after that, then, finally

Prepositional phrases: before (the game), after (the wedding), in (the morning), during (the movie)

Follow these punctuation rules for using commas with time and order signals:

Rules	Examples
If a signal word or phrase comes at the beginning of a sentence, then put a comma after it.	Mary entered her office. **After that,** she switched on the lights.
Do not put a comma after *then*.	Put a scoop of instant coffee in a cup. **Then** pour boiling water over it.
Do not put a comma before a signal word or prepositional phrase at the end of a sentence.	The audience was silent **during the movie**.

Practice 1

Underline the signal word or phrase that has correct punctuation.

Example:

1 *We ate dinner. [Then / Then,] we watched a movie.*

2 Last night Jeremy cleaned up his room. [First / First,] he picked up all his dirty clothes and put them in the laundry. [Then / Then,] he dusted the furniture. [Last / Last,] he vacuumed the rug.

3 My family has lived in several cities. When I was born, we lived in Melbourne, Australia. We moved to Berlin[, after that / after that]. [In 2007 / In 2007,] we bought a house in Rome, and that's where we live[, now / now].

4 I sing in a choir. Our rehearsals are on Thursday nights. [At the beginning / At the beginning,] we sing scales and do exercises to warm up our voices. Our choir director hands out new music[, after that / after that]. We spend the rest of the rehearsal learning the music and practicing it. Singing makes me happy. I'm always in a good mood[, by the end / by the end] of the evening.

Practice 2

Complete each sentence with the signal word or prepositional phrase in parentheses. Add a comma if necessary. Capitalize the first word in the sentence.

Paragraph 1

To make a delicious peanut butter and banana sandwich you will need a plate, a knife, a banana, two slices of bread, and a jar of peanut butter.

1 _____ (first) place the two slices of bread on a plate.

2 _____ (second) use the knife to spread a thick layer of peanut butter on both slices.

3 Peel a banana _____ (after that) and cut it into many thin slices.

4 _____ (then) put the banana slices on top of the peanut butter.

5 _____ (finally) put the two slices of bread together. Your sandwich is ready to eat.

Paragraph 2

My friend Vicki and I had fun exploring downtown Los Angeles yesterday morning.

6 _____ (to begin) we took the subway and got off at Pershing Square.

7 _____ (then) we crossed the street and entered the Biltmore Hotel.

8 _____ (third) we went for a ride on Angel's Flight, which is a cable car that carries people up and down a steep hill.

9 We were hungry _____ (by now) so we walked over to the Grand Central Market and had a delicious Chinese lunch.

10 We visited the Bradbury Building _____ (after lunch).

11 _____ (at 2 p.m.) it was time to go home. We enjoyed our downtown tour very much.

COMMAS WITH TRANSITION SIGNALS

Presentation

Commas with Transition Signals

Transition signals are words and phrases that show relationships between ideas in two complete sentences. They can introduce additional ideas, examples, emphasis, contradictions, similarity, results, and so on.

Common transition signals include:

Additional ideas: *in addition, also, moreover, furthermore*

Contrasting ideas: *however, in contrast, on the other hand, instead*

Emphasis: *in fact, actually, surprisingly*

Examples: *for example, for instance*

Similarity: *similarly*

Results: *therefore, as a result*

Follow these rules for using commas with transition signals:

Rules	Examples
Put a period at the end of the first sentence and a comma after transition signals at the beginning of the second sentence.	Jose speaks Spanish. **However,** he doesn't speak Portuguese.
	Marina goes to school full time. **In addition,** she has a part-time job.
Don't use a comma with *also* when it is in the middle of the sentence.	They keep in touch by email. They **also** use Skype several times a week.
Instead of a comma, you can connect the two sentences with a semicolon. End the first sentence with a semicolon, and begin the second sentence with the transition word followed by a comma. Begin the transition word with a lowercase letter.	Juan speaks Spanish**; however,** he doesn't speak Portuguese.
	We grow many kinds of vegetables**; for example,** we grow tomatoes in the summer.
You can place the transition word or phrase in the middle of the second sentence. Use a comma on both sides of the transition word or phrase.	Juan speaks Spanish. He, **however,** doesn't speak Portuguese.
Some transition words and phrases can end a sentence. They must follow a comma.	Jim likes to travel a lot; his brother prefers to stay home, **however**.

Practice 1

Read the pair of sentences. Circle the letter of the sentence(s) with correct punctuation and capitalization.

Example:

1 **ⓐ** *The house has six bedrooms. However, only two of them have furniture.*
  b *The house has six bedrooms. However only two of them have furniture.*

2 **a** When she got her first job, Gail bought a small apartment. In addition she bought a used car.
  b When she got her first job, Gail bought a small apartment. In addition, she bought a used car.

3 **a** The car broke down three times in three months. therefore, she decided to sell it.
  b The car broke down three times in three months; therefore, she decided to sell it.

4 **a** The apartment was dark and stuffy. Also the neighbors were noisy.
  b The apartment was dark and stuffy. Also, the neighbors were noisy.

5 **a** Gail was unhappy in the apartment; as a result, she decided to sell it.
  b Gail was unhappy in the apartment; As a result she decided to sell it.

6 **a** Susan is a good student. In fact, she is the top student in her class.
  b Susan is a good student. In fact she is the top student in her class.

7 **a** Zelda is a top student. She also participates in several after-school activities.
  b Zelda is a top student. She, also, participates in several after-school activities.

8 **a** Mika was an outstanding student in high school; Therefore, she was accepted to six universities.
  b Mika was an outstanding student in high school; therefore, she was accepted to six universities.

9 **a** Mika was accepted to six universities. None of them, however, offered her a scholarship.
  b Mika was accepted to six universities. None of them however offered her a scholarship.

10 **a** I have a very talented dog. For example, if you throw a ball to him, he can catch it in his mouth.
  b I have a very talented dog. For example if you throw a ball to him, he can catch it in his mouth.

11 **a** Sometimes my dog acts just like a small child. For instance he looks guilty when he does something bad.
  b Sometimes my dog acts just like a small child. For instance, he looks guilty when he does something bad.

Practice 2

The following sentences have been rewritten using the transition signals in parentheses. Circle the letters of the rewritten sentences that have correct punctuation and capitalization. Note: More than one option may be correct.

Example:

1 *An alligator has a wide, round nose. A crocodile's nose is longer and more pointed. (in contrast)*

  ⓐ *An alligator has a wide, round nose. In contrast, a crocodile's nose is longer and more pointed.*

  ⓑ *An alligator has a wide, round nose; in contrast, a crocodile's nose is longer and more pointed.*

  c *An alligator has a wide, round nose in contrast a crocodile's nose is longer and more pointed.*

2 There are more than a million wild American alligators. The Chinese alligator is nearly extinct. (on the other hand)

  a There are more than a million wild American alligators. On the other hand, the Chinese alligator is nearly extinct.

  b There are more than a million wild American alligators on the other hand; the Chinese alligator is nearly extinct.

  c There are more than a million wild American alligators; on the other hand, the Chinese alligator is nearly extinct.

3 Many myths have been told about alligators. Some people believe they can live for hundreds of years. (for example)

  a Many myths have been told about alligators. For example, some people believe they can live for hundreds of years.

  b Many myths have been told about alligators for example some people believe they can live for hundreds of years.

  c Many myths have been told about alligators; for example, some people believe they can live for hundreds of years.

  d Many myths have been told about alligators for example; some people believe they can live for hundreds of years.

4 This is untrue. (however)

  a This is however untrue.

  b However, this is untrue.

  c This is untrue, however.

5 Wild alligators live 30 or 40 years. Alligators in zoos can live 60 to 80 years. (in contrast)

    a Wild alligators live 30 to 40 years, in contrast alligators in zoos can live 60 to 80 years.

    b Wild alligators live 30 to 40 years. In contrast, alligators in zoos can live 60 to 80 years.

    c Wild alligators live 30 to 40 years; in contrast, alligators in zoos can live 60 to 80 years.

6 Crocodiles are found in many countries. They can only live in warm climates. (however)

    a Crocodiles are found in many countries. However, they can only live in warm climates.

    b Crocodiles are found in many countries; however, they can only live in warm climates.

    c Crocodiles are found in many countries. They can only live, however, in warm climates.

    d Crocodiles are found in many countries. They can only live in warm climates, however.

7 There are no crocodiles in Canada, northern Europe, or Russia. (therefore)

    a Therefore, there are no crocodiles in Canada, northern Europe, or Russia.

    b Therefore; there are no crocodiles in Canada, northern Europe, or Russia.

8 There are very few crocodiles in North America. Only about 500 remain. (in fact)

    a There are very few crocodiles in North America. In fact, only about 500 remain.

    b There are very few crocodiles in North America; in fact, only about 500 remain.

    c There are very few crocodiles in North America in fact only about 500 remain.

9 Crocodiles are an endangered species in the United States. (for that reason)

    a For that reason, crocodiles are an endangered species in the United States.

    b For that reason crocodiles are an endangered species in the United States.

COMMAS WITH ADJECTIVE CLAUSES

> ### Presentation
>
> ### Commas with Adjective Clauses
>
> Adjective (relative) clauses modify nouns. They begin with words called relative pronouns. Three of the most common relative pronouns are *who*, *that*, and *which*. Adjective clauses can appear with or without commas.
>
> Follow these rules for using commas with adjective clauses:
>
> | Rules | Examples |
> |---|---|
> | Do not use commas if the adjective clause is necessary to identify the noun it modifies. Use *who*, *that*, or *which* to begin these clauses.

Which is not common in these clauses. Use *that*. | The Smiths want a car **that has room for six people**.
(The adjective clause is necessary to explain which type of car the Smiths want.) |
> | Use *who* in clauses that describe people. Use *that* in clauses that describe things or people. | She is the waitress **who / that served me dinner**. *(The adjective clause is necessary to explain which waitress the sentence is about.)* |
> | Use commas if the identity of the noun is clear without the adjective clause. In this case, the adjective clause adds extra information. Use *who* or *which* to begin these clauses. Do not use *that*. | The Smiths want a Honda minivan, **which has room for six people**.
(The adjective clause is not necessary. We already know which kind of car the Smiths want.) |
> | | Donna, **who served our food**, lives in my neighborhood. *(This is additional information about Donna.)* |

Practice 1

Circle the letter of the sentence that uses commas correctly.

Example:

1 a *The man, who died recently, was a famous writer.*
   (b) *Ray Bradbury, who died recently, was a famous writer.*

2 a Vegetables, that contain beta-carotene, help fight disease.
   b Carrots, which contain beta-carotene, help fight disease.

3 a Drinks, that contain a lot of sugar, cause tooth decay.
   b Soda, which contains a lot of sugar, causes tooth decay.

4 a Ms. Adams, who has young children, doesn't have a lot of time to study.
   b Students, who have young children, don't have a lot of time to study.

5 **a** I refuse to eat at restaurants, that play loud music.

   b I refuse to eat at Mario's Deli, which plays loud music.

6 **a** A room, that has no windows, gets very hot in the summer.

   b My office, which has no windows, gets very hot in the summer.

7 **a** A doctor, who smokes, is not a good role model for his patients.

   b Dr. Chang, who smokes, is not a good role model for his patients.

8 **a** Animals, that live in deserts, can survive for a long time without water.

   b Camels, which live in deserts, can survive for a long time without water.

9 **a** A person, who studies butterflies, is an entomologist.

   b Dr. Evans, who studies butterflies, is an entomologist.

10 **a** Detweiler Beach, which is polluted, is not safe for swimming.

   b A beach, that is polluted, is not safe for swimming.

11 **a** Reiko and Emi, who did not come to class, lied to the teacher about their absence.

   b Students, who do not come to class, lie to the teacher about their absence.

Practice 2

Correct each sentence using commas.

Example:

1 *My birthday is the Fourth of July which is also a national holiday.*

   My birthday is __the Fourth of July,__ *which is also a national holiday.*

2 Belinda who was tired after studying all night fell asleep in class.

   _____ fell asleep in class.

3 Tehran which is the capital of Iran has a population of more than 8 million people.

   _____ has a population of more than 8 million people.

4 Madagascar which is an island in the Indian Ocean has thousands of unique plant and animal species.

   _____ has thousands of unique plant and animal species.

5 I need to make an appointment with Dr. Afar who is my dentist.

   I need to make an appointment with _____ .

6 Great Danes which are large dogs are usually very gentle.

   _____ are usually very gentle.

7 We are flying to Europe on Lufthansa which is a German airline.

   We are flying to Europe on _____ .

8 I enjoy working out at my health club which is open 24 hours.

I enjoy working out at _____ .

9 My favorite dessert is baklava which is a rich Middle Eastern cake filled with nuts and honey.

My favorite dessert is _____ .

10 Let's have the meeting at Jay's house which has a large living room.

Let's have the meeting at _____ .

11 *The King's Speech* which won an Oscar is about King George V of England.

_____ is about King George V of England.

Letters

PUNCTUATION IN LETTERS

Punctuation in Letters

The following rules describe how to use commas in property addresses and in openings and closings of letters.

Rules	Examples
In a sentence, use a comma to separate the street address from the city and the city from the state.	I live at 1157 South Point Street, Los Angeles, California.
Do not place a comma between the state and the zip code.	California 90025
On an envelope, don't write a comma after the street address. Keep the comma after the city name.	1157 South Point Street Los Angeles, California 90025
Use a comma after the greeting in a personal letter.	Dear Aunt Mary,
In a business letter, use a colon after the name if you don't know the person's proper name.	Dear Editor:
	Dear Sir or Madam:
Place a comma after the closing.	Love,
	Sincerely,
	Yours truly,

Practice 1

Review each item. Is the punctuation correct or incorrect? Circle the letter of your answer.

Example:

1 *I can't wait to see you next month.*
   Love
   Mary
   a *Correct*
   (**b**) *Incorrect*

2 Dear Ana,
   Thank you for your recent letter.
   a Correct
   b Incorrect

3 Most of my cousins live in Philadelphia
   Pennsylvania.
   a Correct
   b Incorrect

4 (Address on an envelope)
   Ms. Jane Doe
   255 N. Doheny Drive
   Beverly Hills, CA 90210
   a Correct
   b Incorrect

5 The theater is at 355 Hill St. Detroit
   Michigan 48202
   a Correct
   b Incorrect

6 Dear Sir
   I am writing to inform you. . .
   a Correct
   b Incorrect

7 We look forward to receiving your
   payment.
   Sincerely,
   Roger Brent
   Billing Manager
   a Correct
   b Incorrect

8 The Empire State Building is located at
   350 5th Ave., New York New York 10118.
   a Correct
   b Incorrect

9 I usually buy my fruits and vegetables
   at the market on Pico Boulevard in
   Carlsbad.
   a Correct
   b Incorrect

10 Dear Mr. Sakamoto,

   . . .

   Best wishes
   Linda Rogers
   a Correct
   b Incorrect

11 (on an envelope)
   Mr. Paul Nessen
   12399 Vermont Ave.
   Reno, Nevada, 89001
   a Correct
   b Incorrect

Practice 2

Read the following pairs of openings, closings, and addresses. Which one is correctly punctuated? Circle the letter of your answer.

Example:

1 a *Dear Mrs. Sonata*
  (b) *Dear Mrs. Sonata,*

2 a We have a summer house in Carmel California.
  b We have a summer house in Carmel, California.

3 a The party is at 626 W. Shannon St. Topeka Kansas 66601.
  b The party is at 626 W. Shannon St., Topeka, Kansas 66601.

4 a With best wishes, Paula
  b With best wishes Paula

5 a To Whom It May Concern:
  b To Whom It May Concern

6 (on an envelope)
  a 186 Pleasant St. Brookline Mass. 02146
  b 186 Pleasant St. Brookline, Mass. 02146

7 (on an envelope)
  a 357 Orwell Lane Encinitas, CA 92024
  b 357 Orwell Lane, Encinitas CA 92024

8 (on an envelope)
  a 1600 Pennsylvania Ave., Tacoma, Washington, 20500
  b 1600 Pennsylvania Ave. Tacoma, Washington 20500

9 a Dear Auntie Beth,
  b Dear Auntie Beth:

10 a Please drop off this package at 2845, Main St.
  b Please drop off this package at 2845 Main St.

11 a Sincerely, Janice Kamin
  b Sincerely Janice Kamin

The Sentence
SENTENCE PUNCTUATION

Presentation

A complete sentence has a subject and a verb and expresses a complete thought. Follow these rules for proper capitalization and end punctuation of sentences.

Rules	Examples
Begin every sentence with a capital letter.	**R**oses need a lot of water.
A sentence must have final punctuation, such as a period, a question mark, or an exclamation point.	It's time to turn out the lights.
Questions end in question marks.	Where are my keys**?**
Exclamation points show strong feeling. Use sparingly.	I won first prize in the contest**!**

Practice 1

In each set of sentences, circle the letter of the sentence with correct capitalization and end punctuation.

Example:

1 a *there's a spider in the bathtub.*
  b *There's a spider in the bathtub*
  c *There's a spider in the bathtub.*

2 a my roommate is learning Spanish
  b My roommate is learning Spanish.
  c My roommate is learning Spanish

3 a She is from Russia
  b she is from Russia.
  c She is from Russia.

4 a She already speaks four languages.
  b She already speaks four languages
  c she already speaks four languages

5 **a** How many languages do you speak?

    b how many languages do you speak?

    c How many languages do you speak.

6 **a** My brother learned Chinese in high school.

    b my brother learned Chinese in high school?

    c My brother learned Chinese in high school

7 **a** that is amazing

    b that is amazing!

    c That is amazing!

8 **a** which language is the most similar to English

    b Which language is the most similar to English

    c Which language is the most similar to English?

9 **a** many European languages are related.

    b Many European languages are related.

    c Many European languages are related

10 **a** for example, Dutch is very close to English.

    b For example, Dutch is very close to English

    c For example, Dutch is very close to English.

11 **a** For me, learning languages is incredibly difficult.

    b For me, learning languages is incredibly difficult?

    c for me, learning languages is incredibly difficult.

Practice 2

Rewrite each sentence with a capital letter and end punctuation as needed.

Example:

1 *last Saturday was my thirtieth birthday*

    Last Saturday was my thirtieth birthday.

2 my husband wanted to take me out to dinner

3 He asked me to choose a restaurant

4 I thought about it for a while

5 what kind of food did I feel like eating

6 finally, I chose a French restaurant

7 He made a reservation for seven o'clock

_____

8 he made some other plans as well

_____

9 when we arrived at the restaurant, the host took us to a private room

_____

10 we walked in, and I saw about ten of our friends sitting there

_____

11 it was a huge surprise

_____

Quotations

Presentation

Quotations

A quotation (*quote*) is an exact statement of a person's words. Follow these rules for punctuating quotations.

Rules	Examples
Put quotation marks before and after a person's exact words.	"I'll call you later."
Capitalize the first word of the quote.	"**T**he temperature is 40 degrees Fahrenheit."
Introduce quotations with reporting phrases such as *He said, She asked, The doctor wrote,* and *According to.*	**According to** a government report, "Two-thirds of American children are overweight."
Place a comma after a reporting phrase at the beginning of a quotation.	Robert said**,** "Someday I'm going to be famous."
A reporting phrase can also come after the quotation. Put a comma before it. If the sentence ends with anything other than a period, do not use a comma.	"I'm going to be famous someday," **Robert said**. "Am I going to be famous someday?" **Robert asked**.
Put periods, question marks, and exclamation points before the final quotation mark.	<u>Correct</u>: Jon asked, "What is an armadillo**?**"
	<u>Incorrect</u>: Jon asked, "What is an armadillo"?
If a quoted sentence is divided, then begin the second part with a lowercase letter. Place the reporting phrase in the middle. Use two sets of quotation marks.	"It's not fair," Gail complained, "**t**hat you won't let me borrow the car."

Practice 1

Read the set of sentences. Circle the letter of the sentence with correct punctuation and capitalization.

Example:

1 a *Susan asked "Why is that hat on the floor?"*

  b *Susan asked, "Why is that hat on the floor?"*

  c *Susan asked, "why is that hat on the floor?"*

2 a "Good evening" the restaurant host said.

  b Good evening, the restaurant host said.

  c "Good evening," the restaurant host said.

3 a He asked us, Do you have a reservation?"
  b He asked us, "Do you have a reservation?"
  c He asked us, "do you have a reservation?"

4 a No, we replied, "do we need one?"
  b "No," we replied, "do we need one?"
  c "No, we replied, do we need one?"

5 a "I'm afraid so. We're very full this evening", the host told us.
  b I'm afraid so. We're very full this evening, the host told us.
  c "I'm afraid so. We're very full this evening," the host told us.

6 a The weatherman said, "tomorrow's weather will be cool with a chance of showers.
  b The weatherman said, "Tomorrow's weather will be cool with a chance of showers."
  c The weatherman said, "tomorrow's weather will be cool with a chance of showers."

7 a John asked, "Should we cancel our picnic?"
  b John asked, "Should we cancel our picnic"?
  c John asked "Should we cancel our picnic?"

8 a No, Joyce replied, "but we'd better take our umbrellas."
  b No, Joyce replied, but we'd better take our umbrellas."
  c "No," Joyce replied, "but we'd better take our umbrellas."

9 a Boris asked Zina, "have you ever heard of zydeco music?"
  b Boris asked Zina, "Have you ever heard of zydeco music?"
  c Boris asked Zina, "Have you ever heard of zydeco music"?

10 a She replied, "No, what is it?"
  b She replied, No, what is it?"
  c She replied, "No, what is it?

11 a It's a kind of American folk music from Louisiana, he explained.
  b "It's a kind of American folk music from Louisiana, he explained.
  c "It's a kind of American folk music from Louisiana," he explained.

Practice 2

Rewrite the sentences. Add quotation marks and commas to the quotations.

Example:

1 *The president told the nation The economy is growing stronger.*

   The president told the nation, "The economy is growing stronger."

2 A little boy told his mother Did you know dogs can talk?

   _____

3 Really? What do they say? his mother replied.

   _____

4 The boy said It depends. Big dogs say woof-woof. Little dogs say arf arf.

   _____

5 Spanish dogs have their own language the mother said. They say guau guau.

   _____

6 That's funny the boy said.

   _____

7 The mother added That's not all. Japanese dogs say wan wan, and Israeli dogs say
   hav hav.

   _____

   _____

8 The boy said That's crazy that those dogs speak more languages than I do.

   _____

Paragraph Format

Presentation

Paragraph Format

A paragraph is a group of sentences about one topic. **Format** is the way a paragraph looks on the page. Follow these guidelines when you write an academic paragraph:

- Insert a **heading**. The heading should include your full name, the course you are writing the paragraph for, and the complete date. Place the heading in the upper left-hand corner.

- Include a **title** for your paragraph. Center the title above the paragraph.

- The spaces on the left and right of the typed page are called **margins**. Your left margin should be straight. The right margin does not need to be straight.

- Begin the first line of the paragraph five spaces from the left margin. This is called **indenting**.

- Begin each sentence with a capital letter.

- End each sentence with a **form of punctuation**—a period, question mark, or exclamation mark.

- Leave a blank space between lines. This is called **double-spacing**. Double-spacing makes the paragraph easier to read.

- Insert one space between the end of one sentence and the beginning of the next sentence. When you finish a sentence, continue writing on the same line. This is called **running in**. Don't write each sentence on a separate line.

Example:

Katya Belov
English 100
November 20, 2013

The Amazing Cockroach

Cockroaches have lived on Earth for more than 400 million years. Three characteristics explain this insect's amazing ability to survive. First of all, cockroaches can live almost anywhere—outdoors in tropical climates and indoors in cooler ones. They prefer warm, humid places. For that reason, they are often found in homes and factories where food is prepared and stored. Another characteristic that helps cockroaches survive is that they will eat almost anything. Their diet includes not only human food but also dead insects, paper, and even glue! Finally, cockroaches have few natural enemies. They smell bad, and eating them causes most birds and animals to get sick. These three reasons explain why cockroaches will probably survive on Earth long after most other animals disappear.

Practice 1

Label the paragraph with the correct format features.

Run-in sentences   Straight left margin   Uneven right margin   Indent
Title   Final punctuation   Heading

Katya Belov   1. _____

English 100

November 20, 2013

The Amazing Cockroach   2. _____

3. _____   Cockroaches have lived on Earth for more than

4. _____ 400 million years. Three characteristics explain

this insect's amazing ability to survive. First of all,

cockroaches can live almost anywhere—outdoors

in tropical climates and indoors in cooler ones. They   5. _____

prefer warm, humid places. For that reason, they

are often found in homes and factories where food

is prepared and stored. Another characteristic that

helps cockroaches survive is that they will eat almost

anything. Their diet includes not only human food

but also dead insects, paper, and even glue! Finally,   6. _____

cockroaches have few natural enemies. They smell bad,

and eating them causes most birds and animals to get

sick. These three reasons explain why cockroaches

will probably survive on Earth long after most other

animals disappear.   7. _____

Practice 2

Read the paragraph. Is it formatted correctly or incorrectly? For each item, circle the letter for *Correct* or *Incorrect*.

Marianne Sanders
English 100
November 27, 2013

No Pets on Board!

In my opinion, people should not be allowed to bring pets on airplanes. I have several reasons for my opinion. First, many people are allergic to cats or dogs. If they are sitting near someone's pet on a crowded flight, it might not be possible for them to move to a different seat. They could get sick. Second, pets may disturb human passengers. Dogs in particular can be noisy. They may bark and upset passengers who are trying to read, sleep, or just relax. Third, a pet may escape from its carrier and create a dangerous situation in the plane. One time I was flying to Los Angeles, and a woman took her cat out of its carrier. The cat jumped out of her arms and began running around the plane. I think it was terrified and wanted to find a place to hide. Instead of helping passengers, the flight attendants had to spend time trying to catch the cat. This created an unsafe situation. In summary, these reasons explain why I don't think pets should be allowed to fly as passengers in airplanes.

1 Heading
  a Correct
  b Incorrect

2 Title
  a Correct
  b Incorrect

3 Final punctuation
  a Correct
  b Incorrect

4 Double spacing
  a Correct
  b Incorrect

5 Indentation
  a Correct
  b Incorrect

6 Capital letters
  a Correct
  b Incorrect

7 Left margin
  a Correct
  b Incorrect

8 Right margin
  a Correct
  b Incorrect

9 Run-in sentences
  a Correct
  b Incorrect

GRAMMAR

Adjectives
ADJECTIVES WITH LINKING VERBS

> **Presentation**
>
> Adjectives with Linking Verbs
>
> | Rules | Examples |
> |---|---|
> | Adjectives often occur after linking (or stative) verbs. Linking verbs describe a state or condition, not an action. | The children **are noisy**. |
> | | You **seem confused**. |
> | | Does he **appear sick**? |
> | Common linking verbs are *be, seem, appear, look, smell, taste, sound,* and *feel.* | The garden **looks beautiful**. |
> | | The bread **smells delicious**. |
> | | The soup **tastes salty**. |
> | The adjectives that follow linking verbs describe the subject of a sentence. | A baby's skin **feels smooth**. |

Practice 1

Read each sentence and circle whether it is correct or incorrect.

Example:

1 *After standing on her feet for eight hours, Gina is tired.*

   Incorrect

2 The children don't tired seem.
   Correct
   Incorrect

3 That shirt too small looks.
   Correct
   Incorrect

4 You seem unhappy today.
   Correct
   Incorrect

5 The roses wonderful smell.
   Correct
   Incorrect

6 On a hot day, cold lemonade tastes wonderful.
   Correct
   Incorrect

7 That wool sweater itchy feels.
   Correct
   Incorrect

8 John very tall is.
   Correct
   Incorrect

9 This fish bad tastes.
Correct
Incorrect

11 I don't feel well today.
Correct
Incorrect

10 That answer doesn't right seem.
Correct
Incorrect

Practice 2

Write the words in the correct order to make a complete sentence.

Example:

1 *sweet*   *tastes*   *melon*   .   *The*
<u>The melon tastes sweet</u>.

2 joke   was   funny   .   Cathy's
_____

3 children   sound   happy   .   The
_____

4 cat   lazy   My   .   is
_____

5 teacher   tired   .   seems   Our
_____

6 is   .   weather   The   terrible
_____

7 .   The   soft   grass   feels
_____

8 is   .   old   watch   This
_____

9 .   easy   job   That   looks
_____

10 air   .   The   smells   bad
_____

11 doesn't   The   fresh   milk   .   smell
_____

ADJECTIVE ORDER AND FORM

Presentation

Adjective Order and Form

Rules	Examples
Adjectives describe or give information about nouns. They answer the following questions: *What kind? Which one? How many?*	a **new** car, a **soft** banana *(What kind?)*
	the **third** chapter, **my** uncle *(Which one?)*
	six kittens, **many** mistakes *(How many?)*
Adjectives occur before nouns they describe or after linking verbs such as *be, seem,* or *feel.*	**big** house
	The house is **big**.
Adjectives do not change depending on the noun.	<u>Correct:</u> the **big** house <u>Incorrect:</u> the bigs houses
You can use as many adjectives as you want before a noun in one sentence. In sentences with more than one adjective, the adjectives have to follow a certain order. Here is the order adjectives follow in a sentence:	**beautiful African** dresses
	a **square wood** box
	six old Chinese gold coins
	fun summer activities
Quantity	two, many, a lot of
Opinion	beautiful, confusing, friendly
Size	short, huge, tiny
Shape	square, round, circular
Age	old, young, new
Color	blue, green, dark
Origin	American, African, Indian
Material	wood, porcelain, glass
Noun used as adjective	coffee (cup), wedding (dress)

Practice 1

Circle the 15 adjectives in the paragraph.

I have a very old porcelain coffee mug that I love. It looks ordinary, but it's very special to me because I've had it for more than twenty years. It is white, and it has a faded photo of my daughter on the side. I got it as a birthday present when she was a little girl. The mug is just the right size, and it has a comfortable handle. There's a small crack in the handle, but I don't care. My mug is in bad condition, but I like it because it brings back happy memories whenever I use it.

Practice 2

Write the adjectives in the correct order.

Example:

1 *She loves <u>small</u> <u>round</u> earrings.*
  round   small

2 My family is from Greece, so, when my cousin got married last week,
  she had a _____ _____ _____ wedding.
  traditional   church   Greek

3 She wore a _____ _____ _____ gown.
  silk   gorgeous   white

4 The gown had a _____ _____ train.
  lace   long

5 The groom also comes from a _____ _____ family.
  large   Greek

6 He wore a _____ _____ _____ suit.
  gray   silk   formal

7 The afternoon wedding was followed by a _____ _____ party in the evening.
  huge   loud

8 The guests talked, laughed, sang, danced, and ate _____ _____ _____ food.
  Greek   delicious   a lot of

9 I loved seeing my _____ _____ _____ grandmother dancing with the groom.
  old   tiny   Greek

10 My cousin received _____ _____ _____ gifts.
  wonderful   many   wedding

11 Her favorite gift was a pair of _____ _____ _____ candlesticks that she
  got from our grandmother.
  antique   tall   silver

COMPOUND ADJECTIVES, NOUN ADJECTIVES, PROPER ADJECTIVES

Presentation

Compound Adjectives, Noun Adjectives, Proper Adjectives

Adjective Types	Descriptions	Examples
Compound adjectives	Two or more words that function together to modify a noun. Compound adjectives are usually written with hyphens.	a three-pound chicken, a full-time job, a well-known actor
Noun adjectives	Nouns that are used to describe other nouns. Nouns as adjectives never take a plural form.	wedding dress, football game, computer program (_Incorrect:_ computers programs)
Proper adjectives	Adjectives that refer to names of languages, nationalities, or places. They begin with capital letters.	American flag, Arabic poem, Mexican food

Practice 1

Identify the type of each underlined adjective. Circle the letter of the correct answer.

Example:

1 _Australia is an <u>English-speaking</u> country._

   (a) _compound adjective_
   b _noun adjective_
   c _proper adjective_

2 The restaurant is known for serving <u>16-ounce</u> steaks.

   a compound adjective
   b noun adjective
   c proper adjective

3 Our dog is an <u>Irish</u> setter.
  a compound adjective
  b noun adjective
  c proper adjective

4 Please don't put your feet on the <u>coffee</u> table.
  a compound adjective
  b noun adjective
  c proper adjective

5 Carl drives a <u>two-seat</u> sports car.
  a compound adjective
  b noun adjective
  c proper adjective

6 There's a huge scratch on the <u>computer</u> screen.
  a compound adjective
  b noun adjective
  c proper adjective

7 Esther tried a new kind of <u>Chinese</u> tea.
  a compound adjective
  b noun adjective
  c proper adjective

8 Hye Sook makes beautiful <u>flower</u> arrangements.
  a compound adjective
  b noun adjective
  c proper adjective

9 That club has the best <u>dance</u> floor in the city.
  a compound adjective
  b noun adjective
  c proper adjective

10 Hiro speaks English with a <u>Japanese</u> accent.
  a compound adjective
  b noun adjective
  c proper adjective

11 I asked my roommate to drive me to the <u>train</u> station.
  a compound adjective
  b noun adjective
  c proper adjective

Practice 2

Circle the letter of the correct answer to complete the sentence.

Example:

1 *I love* _____ .

   a *french food*

   ⓑ *French food*

   c *French-food*

2 The U.S. has a _____ .

   a two day weekend

   b two-day weekend

   c Two-Day weekend

3 Have you ever tasted an _____?

   a english muffin

   b English muffin

   c English-muffin

4 My little brother loves _____ .

   a peanut butter

   b Peanut butter

   c peanut-butter

5 I have a _____ .

   a ten speed bike

   b ten-speed bike

   c Ten-Speed bike

6 Michiko read a _____ in one weekend.

   a three hundred page book

   b Three Hundred Page book

   c three-hundred-page book

7 Tom drinks a glass of _____ every morning.

   a grapefruit juice

   b Grapefruit juice

   c grapefruit-juice

8 In Kentucky they raise _____ .

   a arabian racehorses

   b Arabian racehorses

   c Arabian-racehorses

9 My father is a _____ .
    a self educated man
    b self-educated man
    c Self-Educated man

10 I forgot to return my _____ .
    a library book
    b Library book
    c library-book

11 I read that _____ are very intelligent.
    a australian sheepdogs
    b Australian sheepdogs
    c Australian-sheepdogs

COMPARATIVE ADJECTIVES

Presentation

Comparative Adjectives

Comparative adjectives show how two people, places, things, or ideas are different. Comparative adjectives are usually followed by *than*.

Follow these rules to form comparative adjectives.

Rules	Examples	Sentences
Add *-er* to one-syllable adjectives. If the adjective ends in vowel + consonant, then double the consonant.	strong > stronger short > shorter fat > fatter	Superman is **stronger than** Spider-Man.
Add *-ier* to two-syllable adjectives that end in *y*. Omit *y*.	easy > easier funny > funnier shy > shyer *(exception)*	Dogs are **funnier than** cats.
Use *more* or *less* in front of adjectives that have two or more syllables.	more colorful, less expensive	A parrot is **more colorful than** a crow. Silver is **less expensive than** gold.
Good, bad, and *far* have irregular comparative forms.	good > better	My new cell phone is **better than** my old one.
	bad > worse	Joe's cooking is **worse than** Ted's.
	far > farther	My brother walked to the **farther** side of town.

Practice 1

Circle the ten comparative adjectives in the paragraph.

Duncan and Jeremy are brothers, but they are different in many ways. First of all, they look very different from one another. Duncan is taller and more muscular than Jeremy. He plays a lot of sports. In contrast, Jeremy has darker eyes and curlier hair than Duncan. The brothers also have very different personalities. Duncan is funnier and more easygoing than Jeremy. He's also more talkative than his brother. In contrast, Jeremy is more creative than Duncan. For example, he likes to write short stories. Jeremy is more organized, and he is a better student.

Practice 2

Complete each sentence. Use the comparative form of the adjective in parentheses and *than*.

Example:

1 *Gold is <u>more expensive than</u> (expensive) silver.*

2 For me, reading is _____ (easy) writing in English.

3 Skiing is _____ (dangerous) swimming.

4 My shoes were _____ (expensive) my dress.

5 The Himalayas are _____ (tall) the Alps.

6 Nightlife in New York is _____ (exciting) nightlife in Boston.

7 The weather in California is _____ (good) the weather in Vermont.

8 Today Sima's cold is _____ (bad) it was yesterday.

9 Richard is _____ (short) his sister.

10 Mara's bedroom is _____ (messy) her sister's.

11 Horses are _____ (intelligent) cows.

SUPERLATIVE ADJECTIVES

Presentation

Superlative Adjectives

Superlative adjectives are used to compare one person, thing, or place with a group of other people, things, or places. A superlative adjective tells us what person, place, thing, animal, or idea has the most or the least of something. Superlative adjectives are preceded by the word _the_.

Follow these rules to form comparative adjectives.

Rules	Examples	Sentences
Use _the_ + adjective + _-est_ for one-syllable adjectives. If the adjective ends in vowel + consonant, then double the consonant.	strong > the strongest fat > the fattest	**The oldest** door in England is in Westminster Abbey.
Use _the_ + adjective + _-iest_ for two-syllable adjectives that end in _y_. Omit _y_.	easy > the easiest shy > the shyest _(exception)_	In my opinion, Jerry Seinfeld is **the funniest** American comedian.
Use _the most_ or _the least_ before adjectives that have two or more syllables.	the most interesting, the least expensive	Many people think that Paris is **the most beautiful** city in the world. I disagree and think it is **the least beautiful** city.
Good, bad, and _far_ have irregular superlative forms.	good > best bad > worst far > farthest	Buffalo, New York, has **the worst** winter weather in the United States.

Practice 1

Circle the letter of the correct form of the superlative in each sentence.

Example:

1 _My name is Lisa. I have three brothers. I am _____ child in my family._
   a _older than_
   b _oldest_
   (c) _the oldest_

2 That restaurant makes _____ hamburgers in the city.
   a greasiest
   b most greasiest
   c the greasiest

3 During a tornado, _____ place to be is underground.
  a most safe
  b safest
  c the safest

4 In my opinion, Steven Spielberg is _____ living movie director.
  a best
  b the best
  c the bestest

5 Dr. Panush is _____ dentist I have ever had.
  a carefulest
  b most careful
  c the most careful

6 That cherry tree is _____ tree in the park.
  a more beautiful than
  b the most beautiful
  c the most beautifulest

7 In my opinion, broccoli has _____ taste of any vegetable.
  a the worst
  b worst
  c worstest

8 In the United States, _____ baby names in 2011 were Sophia for girls and Jacob for boys.
  a most popular
  b popularest
  c the most popular

9 Wednesday was _____ day last week.
  a cloudiest
  b the cloudiest
  c the most cloudy

10 That is _____ recipe in the cookbook.
  a most complicated
  b the complicated
  c the most complicated

11 Who is _____ singer in your country?
  a most famous
  b the famous
  c the most famous

Practice 2

Complete each sentence. Use the superlative form of the adjective in parentheses.

Example:

1 *Singapore is* <u>the cleanest</u> *(clean) city in the world.*

2 Everest is _____ (tall) mountain in the world.

3 The Don Juan Pond in Antarctica is _____ (salty) body of water in the world.

4 The Formula Rossa in Abu Dhabi is _____ (fast) roller coaster in the world.

5 _____ (popular) street name in the United States is "Second St."

6 Tokyo, Japan, is _____ (populated) city on earth.

7 Tokyo is also _____ (expensive) city in the world.

8 _____ (bad) food I ever ate was on a ten-day camping trip in the desert.

9 Istanbul, Turkey, is one of _____ (amazing) cities I've ever seen.

10 I think Schiphol, in Amsterdam, is _____ (good) airport in the world.

11 The Hartsfield–Jackson Atlanta International Airport is _____ (busy) airport in the world.

Adverbs

ADVERBS OF MANNER

Adverbs of Manner

Adverbs modify or give more information about verbs. English has different kinds of adverbs. Adverbs of manner tell *how* something happens.

For example: *The children laughed* **loudly.**

- Adverbs of manner cannot come between the verb and the object.

Incorrect: *She made neatly the bed.*

Correct: *She made the bed neatly.*

- Most adverbs of manner are formed by adding *–ly* to an adjective (*sad – sadly, quiet – quietly*). A few adverbs have the same form as adjectives: *fast, high, low, hard, late, early.*

Correct: *Martina jogs fast.*

Incorrect: *Martina jogs fastly.*

- Some adverbs of manner are not formed by adding *–ly* to the adjectives. The adverb form of *good* is *well.*

- Adverbs of manner can appear in different places in the sentence. Study the chart.

Rules	Examples
We can use adverbs of manner after the verb.	The car stopped **suddenly**.
We can use adverbs of manner before the verb.	She **quickly** closed the door.
We can use adverbs of manner at the beginning of the sentence (followed by a comma).	**Sadly,** she put the photograph in the box.
Adverbs of manner can also come at the end of the sentence.	The old man stood up **slowly**.

Practice 1

Underline the adverb in each sentence.

1 Anita can be very loud. So, when she heard the news, she screamed loudly.

2 Lisa is usually a fast writer. During the test yesterday, she wrote fast, but she did not have enough time to finish the test.

3 The table was beautifully set with my mother's finest dishes and silverware, and decorated with gorgeous flowers.

4 The actor was very good. We could hear him clearly.

5 My cat can be very annoying. Last night, he suddenly jumped onto the table and scared me.

6 Maria's son politely asked for another piece of pie. He is such a polite boy.

7 In the morning, the weather was lovely, but slowly the sky turned dark, and it began to rain.

8 He tried hard, but he couldn't finish the assignment. The assignment was just too hard.

9 Ben seemed upset, and he spoke to his friend quietly.

10 The movie ended sadly. People were silent as they left the theater.

11 Joe was late. Impatiently, he waited for the bus to arrive.

Practice 2

Write the correct adverb of manner to complete each sentence.

seriously	badly	quickly
successfully	silently	

1 David _____ completed his doctorate in physics. Isn't that great?

2 Regina was _____ injured in a car accident last month. However, she is recovering _____ .

3 A: I hear you're studying Russian. How's it going?
B: Well, I can read and write pretty well. But I speak _____ . It's a hard language.

4 The cat approached the bird _____ and jumped.

late	well	fast
slowly	heavily	

5 Our teacher talks too _____ . We asked her to speak more _____ .

6 People tell me that I'm a good singer. When they say I sing _____ , I feel happy.

7 It was raining very _____ this morning, so we cancelled our picnic.

8 Miyuki's plane arrived two hours _____ .

ADVERBS OF FREQUENCY

Presentation

Adverbs of Frequency

Adverbs modify or give additional information about verbs. Adverbs of frequency tell us *how often* something happens.

Example: *Marilyn* **never** *goes anywhere without her phone.*

Some common adverbs of frequency are *always, usually, often, frequently, sometimes, occasionally, rarely, seldom,* and *never.*

Here are some general rules for placing adverbs of frequency in a sentence:

Rules	Examples
Adverbs of frequency usually come before the main verb.	Cora **often** takes the train to work.
	She **sometimes** rides her bike.
	She **never** walks.
Adverbs of frequency usually come after *be*.	Manolo is **never** late.
	Mr. Canning is **seldom** angry.
Some adverbs of frequency can come at the beginning or end of the sentence. These adverbs include *usually, frequently, sometimes, occasionally,* and *often*.	**Frequently** the train is late.
	David works at home **sometimes**.

Practice 1

Read the sets of three sentences. One sentence in each set is incorrect. Circle the letter of the incorrect sentence.

1 **a** She is seldom late.
   b Never she is late.
   c Occasionally she is late.

2 **a** Joanna eats dessert occasionally.
   b Joanna always eats dessert.
   c Joanna eats dessert never.

3 **a** Paul takes sometimes the bus to work.
   b Paul often takes the bus to work.
   c Paul takes the bus to work frequently.

4 a Kazu takes occasionally an 8:00 a.m. class.

b Kazu never takes an 8:00 a.m. class.

c Sometimes Kazu takes an 8:00 a.m. class.

5 a Dr. Magnus usually eats breakfast at home.

b Dr. Magnus often eats breakfast at home.

c Dr. Magnus eats breakfast at home rarely.

6 a Roi sends often text messages during class.

b Roi sometimes sends text messages during class.

c Roi usually sends text messages during class.

7 a Taxi drivers in my town are often rude.

b Taxi drivers in my town never are rude.

c Occasionally, taxi drivers in my town are rude.

8 a Sandra seldom jogs at night.

b Sandra jogs at night sometimes.

c Sandra often jogs at night often.

9 a It usually rains in June.

b Sometimes it rains in June.

c It rains rarely in June.

10 a Ella rarely makes spelling mistakes.

b Ella makes often spelling mistakes.

c Ella sometimes makes spelling mistakes.

11 a Jim sometimes has trouble falling asleep.

b Jim never has trouble falling asleep.

c Jim has frequently trouble falling asleep.

Practice 2

Rewrite each sentence using the adverb of frequency in parentheses. Pay attention to the correct placement of the adverb in each sentence.

Example:

1 *Georgia is late to work. (never)*

Georgia is never late to work.

2 When I was a child, my family ate dinner together. (always)

When I was a child, _____ .

3 My father came home from work at 5 p.m. (usually)

_____ from work at 5 p.m.

4 These days many families eat dinner together because everyone is so busy. (rarely)

These days _____ because everyone is so busy.

5 My wife and I both work very hard. I am home before 7 p.m. (never)

My wife and I both work very hard. _____ before 7 p.m.

6 My wife has to work late, too. (often)

_____ .

7 My kids have activities after school. (usually)

_____ activities after school.

8 They get together with friends to study. (frequently)

_____ with friends to study.

9 However, we have dinner together on Friday nights. (always)

However, _____ together on Friday nights.

10 On weekends, we have a family breakfast. (sometimes)

On weekends, _____ .

11 We go out to brunch. (often)

_____ .

Future

FUTURE WITH BE GOING TO AND WILL

Presentation

Future with *Be going to* and *Will*

You can talk about the future with *will* and *be going to*. Common time expressions with the future include *tomorrow, next week /month /year, later, soon, tonight, in ten minutes,* and *in just a moment.*

- To talk about **predictions** (**guesses**) or **general future events,** use *will* or *be going to.*

Prediction (guess): I think you will love this restaurant. / I think you are going to love this restaurant.

Future event: The concert will take place in June. / The concert is going to take place in June.

- To express a **promise** or **offer,** use *will.*

Promise: I'll send you an email later today.

Offer: I'll carry those suitcases for you.

- To talk about **plans that have already been made,** use *be going to.*

Sharon is going to graduate in June.

I'm going to buy a new car.

- To talk about **actions that were not planned (or plans that were made at the time of speaking),** use *will*.

A: There's a concert tonight.

B: Really? I think I'll go.

Rules	Examples
To form sentences with *will*, use subject + *will (not)* + base form of the verb.	The **flight will depart** at 11 p.m.
	It **will not rain** tonight.
You can contract the pronoun with *will* in affirmative statements: pronoun + *'ll* + base form of the verb.	**I'll help** you with your homework. **You'll need** to show your passport.
	He'll carry these bags for me.
	She'll be here soon.
	It'll be just fine.
	We'll wait for you in the arrivals hall.
You can contract the pronoun with *will* in negative statements: pronoun + *won't* + base form of the verb.	**I won't** be at the airport.
	You won't arrive on time.
	We won't have time to eat.
To form sentences with *be going to*, use subject + *be (am, are, is)* + *(not) going to* + base form of the verb. Make sure that the form of *be* agrees with the subject.	**He is going to get** married soon.
	We are not going to attend the wedding.
You can use contractions with *be*: pronoun + *'m / 're / 's* + *(not) going to* + base form of the verb.	**I'm going to take** some time off work.
	She's going to have lunch with her mother.
	We're not going to buy that car.
Another way to use contractions with *be*: pronoun + *aren't / isn't* + *going to* + base form of the verb.	**She isn't going to have** lunch with her mother.
	We aren't going to buy that car.

Practice 1

Circle the letter of the correct form of the future tense to complete each sentence.

Example:

1 *In fifty years, the world* _____ *more than 9 billion people.*
   a *have*
   b *will has*
   ⓒ *is going to have*

2 Most of those people _____ in Africa and South Asia.
   a are going to live
   b will to live
   c going to live

3 Cities _____ very crowded.
   a be
   b going to be
   c will be

4 There probably _____ enough fresh water.
  a willn't be
  b won't be
  c not going to be

5 Some countries that exist today _____ in fifty years.
  a not exist
  b won't going to exist
  c aren't going to exist

6 I am sure that doctors _____ a cure for most types of cancer.
  a going to find
  b will find
  c will to find

7 Nobody _____ cash anymore.
  a going to use
  b will to use
  c will use

8 People _____ for everything with their phones.
  a are going to pay
  b going to pay
  c pay

9 I hope there _____ any more wars.
  a not going to be
  b won't be
  c not be

10 Because of global warming, the level of the oceans _____ .
  a is rise
  b will to rise
  c is going to rise

11 My house is next to the beach. In fifty years, it _____ underwater.
  a be
  b going to be
  c is going to be

Practice 2

Complete each sentence with *will* or *be going to* and the verb in parentheses. Sometimes both forms are correct, but you should write only one.

1 Jay Singh _____ (graduate) from Harvard Medical School on May 20, 2018. His parents and his brother _____ (come) to his graduation ceremony. It _____ (be) their first trip outside of India. Unfortunately, his sister _____ (not come) because she has small children. "We _____ (take) lots of pictures of the ceremony," promised her parents.

2 **Vivian:** My car broke down, and my family is flying in tonight. I'm not sure what to do.

Mark: Don't worry. I _____ (lend) you my car. I'm happy to help.

Vivian: Thanks! But don't you need it?

Mark: No, I don't. I have a lot of work to do, so I _____ (stay) home and study.

3 **Kim:** Hi, Sandor? This is Kim. I'm at your house. I need to borrow a ladder.

Sandor: I'm at the gym now. I _____ (not be) home for a while.

Kim: That's OK. I _____ (wait) for you.

Sandor: Fine. But why do you need a ladder?

Kim: There's a mouse in my attic. I want to trap it, but I need a ladder to get up there.

Sandor: OK. You can borrow my ladder. But I _____ (not help) you catch the mouse.

Kim: Why not? Are you afraid of heights?

Sandor: No, I'm afraid of mice!

Kim: Ha ha! OK, I promise I _____ (not ask) you to catch it!

FUTURE REAL CONDITIONAL

> **Presentation**
>
> ### Future Real Conditional
>
> Sentences with the future real conditional talk about what will happen under certain conditions. The future real conditional has two parts (clauses). The *if*-clause gives the condition. The main clause describes the possible future result of the condition: what may, will, or won't happen.
>
> **Example:** If I have time, I'll visit my sister tomorrow. (*It's a real possibility that I will have time. Having time is the condition under which I will visit my sister.*)
>
> Follow these rules for the correct use of the future real conditional.
>
> | Rules | Examples |
> |---|---|
> | The *if*-clause can come before or after the main clause. If it comes first, then put a comma after it. | **If I have time,** then I'll visit my sister tomorrow. |
> | | I'll visit my sister tomorrow **if I have time**. |
> | Use the simple present in the *if*-clause. | **If you pay for dinner**, I'll pay for the movie. |
> | Use the future with *will* or *be going to* in the main clause. | If you are not ready, **I'm going to leave without you**. |
> | One or both clauses can be negative. | **If you don't hurry**, we're going to miss the bus. |
> | | **If you don't study**, **you won't get good grades**. |

Practice 1

Circle the form of the verb that correctly completes each sentence.

Example:

1 *If I (have / will have) time, I (meet / will meet) you for lunch.*

2 If the weather (is / will be) good, we (go / will go) for a hike.

3 John has been sick for three days. If he (doesn't feel / will not feel) better tomorrow, he (goes / will go) to the doctor.

4 The water in the river is polluted. You (get / will get) sick if you (drink / will drink) it.

5 James (doesn't graduate / won't graduate) if he (won't pass / doesn't pass) his last exam.

6 If you (don't have / won't have) any questions, I (will go / go) help someone else.

7 My computer is old. If it (breaks down / will break down), I (buy / am going to buy) a new one.

8 The flowers (die / will die) if you (aren't going to water / don't water) them.

9 Morris (apply / will apply) to law school if he (doesn't find / won't find) a job soon.

10 If you (are / will be) late, I (don't wait / won't wait) for you.

11 I (won't buy / don't buy) the shoes if they (don't fit / won't fit) perfectly.

Practice 2

Complete each sentence with the correct form of the verbs in parentheses.

Example:

1 *If I <u>see</u> (see) Ali in class, I'<u>ll give</u> (give) him your message.*

2 If you _____ (not like) this jacket, I _____ (take) it back to the store.

3 The children need to play quietly. They _____ (wake up) Grandpa if they _____ (make) too much noise.

4 If you _____ (not agree) with my suggestion, I _____ (think) of a better one.

5 I _____ (come) back tomorrow if you _____ (be) too busy to see me today.

6 If you _____ (finish) your homework early, I _____ (take) you bowling.

7 The teacher _____ (repeat) the instructions if the students _____ (not understand) them.

8 If I _____ (not do) the laundry today, I _____ (not have) any clean clothes to wear to work.

9 If I _____ (take) a nap now, I _____ (not be) able to fall asleep tonight.

10 If you _____ (not mail) the package today, it _____ (not arrive) before the holidays.

11 We _____ (not go) fishing if it _____ (rain) tomorrow.

Imperatives

Presentation

Imperatives

Imperatives are sentences that give commands, advice, directions, warnings, or instructions. You can also use imperatives to make requests or invitations. The imperative sentence (or clause) begins with the base form of the verb, but the understood subject is always *you*. Use *please* to make imperatives more polite. Remember that the imperative form is the same in both the singular and the plural.

Forms	Examples
Affirmative	**Please sit** down.
	Take the plates and **put** them on the table.
	Exercise to be healthy.
	Be careful!
Negative	**Don't / Do not call** them after 9.
	Don't / Do not forget to turn off the light.
	Please don't / do not sing so loud.
	Don't / Do not fall!

Practice 1

Read the paragraph. Underline ten imperatives.

It's very easy to make popcorn in a microwave oven. To begin, place the bag of popcorn in the center of the microwave. Look for the words "this side up" on the bag so that you will know which way to place the bag. Next, set the timer on your microwave oven for two minutes and thirty seconds and press the "Start" button. Don't leave the room while the popcorn is popping. You need to stay nearby and listen. When the popping slows down to one or two seconds between pops, stop the microwave to prevent burning. Remove the bag from the microwave and open it very slowly. It will be very hot! When it is cool enough, pour the popcorn into a bowl and enjoy eating it.

Practice 2

Choose words from the box to complete the sentences with imperatives.

find	park	stop	turn on
go	remain	touch	use
keep	stay		

According to the National Weather Service, lightning causes an average of 62 deaths and 300 injuries in the United States each year. To stay safe during a lightning storm, follow these instructions.

If you are indoors,

<u>don't use</u> the phone. (But cell phones are safe to use.)

_____ away from windows.

_____ the water. If lightning hits your house, the electricity can travel into the house through the metal pipes.

If you are driving,

_____ the car.

_____ in an open area, away from trees and power poles.

_____ any metal objects in the car.

_____ in the car until the storm passes.

If you are outdoors,

_____ shelter inside a building, if possible.

_____ away from trees, tall objects, and water. They "attract" the lightning.

_____ near metal fences, gates, power poles, etc. The electricity from the lightning travels through metal.

Modals

CAN, CAN'T, COULD, AND COULDN'T

Presentation

Modals: Can, Can't, Could, and Couldn't

Modal verbs are different from regular verbs:

- They have only one form, without –s or –ed.
- They are followed by the base form of the verb.

The modals *can* and *could* are used to talk about:

- ability in the present (*can*) and past (*could*)
- possibility in the present and future

To form a negative with *can* and *could*, use **can / could + not.** You can also use contractions: **cannot – can't, could not – couldn't.**

Study the forms and meanings of these modals.

Time	Ability	Possibility
Present / Future	John **can** swim.	It **could / can** rain this afternoon.
	Betsy **can't / cannot** cook.	I **can / could** stop by your house later.
	Can Andrew sing?	
Past	When I was a child, I **could** speak Korean.	*(none)*
	I **could not / couldn't** drive a car.	

Practice 1

Complete each sentence using *can, can't, could,* or *couldn't.*

Example:

1 I <u>can</u> speak three languages now, but when I was a child, I <u>could</u> only speak one.

2 In the state of California, you _____ get a driver's license when you are 16 years old. Many teens celebrate their 16th birthday by taking their driving test.

3 According to California law, teenage drivers _____ drive passengers under age 20 for the first 12 months.

4 Last year, my friends and I took a vacation in California. We planned to rent a car at the airport. Unfortunately, the agent at the car rental desk told us we had to be 25 to rent a car. As a result, we _____ rent a car.

5 **A:** What would you like to do tonight?

   B: Well, we haven't watched TV all week. We _____ make popcorn and watch a movie.

6 These days, children as young as two _____ use a computer.

7 Mary _____ reach the dishes on the top shelf now because she is too short.

8 I'm sorry I _____ call you last night. I lost your phone number.

9 In San Francisco, it _____ be cold and rainy in the summer. If you go there in June or July, be sure to take an umbrella.

10 When I was a small child I _____ eat with a fork.

11 **Manager:** _____ you finish this project by 5 o'clock?

   Worker: It's possible. If it looks like I _____ finish, I'll let you know.

Practice 2

Each sentence has an error. Rewrite the sentence correctly.

Example:

1 *Alberto cans speaks English very well.*

   <u>Alberto can speak English very well</u>.

2 Please turn down the television. I'm trying to study, and I can't to concentrate.

   Please turn down the television. I'm trying to study, _____ .

3 If you go to the party, you can meets my sister.

   If you go to the party, _____ .

4 I couldn't opened the door because I locked my keys in the car.

   _____ because I locked my keys in the car.

5 Could you to use a computer when you were eight years old?

   _____ when you were eight years old?

6 When Joe went to the library yesterday, he can't remember the name of the book he wanted to borrow.

   When Joe went to the library yesterday, _____ the name of the book he wanted to borrow.

7 Pierre is from France. He has been in the United States for three years. Before he came here, he cannot speak any English. Now he can speak fluently.

Pierre is from France. He has been in the United States for three years. Before he came here, _____ speak any English. Now he can speak fluently.

8 It's a beautiful, sunny morning, but it coulds rain later.

It's a beautiful, sunny morning, but _____ later.

9 I couldn't leave the house right now. I'm expecting an important phone call.

_____ right now. I'm expecting an important phone call.

10 When Mr. Aguilar was a young man, he could ran a mile in six minutes.

When Mr. Aguilar was a young man, _____ in six minutes.

11 Please don't drop that antique vase. If it breaks, I cans not replace it.

Please don't drop that antique vase. If it breaks, _____ .

SHOULD, OUGHT TO, AND HAD BETTER

Modals: *Should, Ought to,* and *Had Better*

Modal verbs are different from regular verbs:

- They have only one form, without –*s* or –*ed.*
- They are followed by the base form of the verb.

Use ***should*** and ***ought to*** to give advice or suggestions in the present and the future.

- *Should* and *ought to* are similar in meaning. *Should* is more common.
- To form the negative, use ***should not / ought not to* + base form** of the verb.

You can use a contraction ***shouldn't / oughtn't.***

- The negative of *ought to* is usually not used in American English.

Use ***had better*** for strong advice. *Had better* is more threatening and urgent than *should / ought to.* It means there will be a bad result if the advice is not followed.

- To form the negative, use ***had better not* + base form** of the verb.
- *Had better* is usually contracted to **'d better** (*I'd better, you'd better, he'd/she'd better, we'd better, they'd better*).

Forms	Examples
should, should not / shouldn't, ought to	You **should / ought to** get more exercise.
	You **shouldn't** drink coffee at night.
had better / 'd better, had better not / 'd better not	We're almost out of gas. We'**d better** stop at a gas station.
	I need to study this evening. I'**d better not** go out.

Practice 1

Read the situation. On the next page, circle the letter for the best advice.

Example:

1 *I have a big test tomorrow.*
  a *You should go out.*
  ⓑ *You'd better study.*
  c *You shouldn't study.*

2 Jeffrey is allergic to peanuts.

   a He'd better not eat peanuts.

   b He should eat peanuts.

   c He ought to eat peanuts.

3 Tina has had three car accidents.

   a She should take some driving lessons.

   b She shouldn't have an accident.

   c She'd better drive.

4 There's no food in the house. Our friends are coming over for dinner.

   a We should invite them.

   b We'd better go shopping.

   c We shouldn't get food.

5 John has trouble falling asleep at night.

   a He should worry.

   b He'd better go to bed.

   c He shouldn't drink coffee in the evening.

6 We are going hiking tomorrow. It's going to be a hot day.

   a We'd better take lots of water.

   b We shouldn't make plans.

   c We shouldn't be thirsty.

7 It rained all week, but it's a beautiful day today.

   a You'd better take an umbrella.

   b You should walk to work.

   c You shouldn't go outside.

8 Mr. Mohsen weighs 300 pounds.

   a He should eat more.

   b He'd better go on a diet.

   c He shouldn't exercise.

9 Mrs. Tippett always gives us terrible advice.

   a We ought to follow her advice.

   b We shouldn't follow her advice.

   c We had better give her advice.

10 Tomorrow is Valentine's Day. Ms. Ang is expecting flowers from her boyfriend.

   a He'd better not forget to buy flowers.

   b He ought to get her some candy.

   c He should forget Valentine's Day.

11 Paul bought a new plasma TV set. He does not know how to turn it on.

   a He'd better not buy a TV.

   b He should read the instruction manual.

   c He shouldn't watch TV.

Practice 2

Correct the errors in the sentences below by filling in the blanks.

Example:

1 *The house is dirty. I should to clean it.*
The house is dirty. I should clean it.

2 If you want to learn English well, you should to come to class every day.
If you want to learn English well, _____ every day.

3 You hadn't better cross the street if the light is red.
_____ the street if the light is red.

4 We shouldn't not waste water.

_____ .

5 On this street, parking is allowed between 8 a.m. and 6 p.m. It's 7 p.m. We had better park here.
On this street, parking is allowed between 8 a.m. and 6 p.m. It's
7 p.m. _____ .

6 When you go to San Francisco, you ought to visiting Chinatown.
When you go to San Francisco, _____ Chinatown.

7 That's a dangerous part of town. You shouldn't not go there alone.
That's a dangerous part of town. _____ alone.

8 I'm going to be late. You shouldn't waiting for me.
I'm going to be late. _____ .

9 If you're going to Paris in December, you had better to take a warm coat.
If you're going to Paris in December, _____ a warm coat.

10 If you want to get tickets for the Lady Gaga concert, you hads better buy them soon. Her shows always sell out fast.
If you want to get tickets for the Lady Gaga concert, _____ them soon. Her shows always sell out fast.

11 It's Mr. Fisk's turn to pick up his kids from school. He had better to not forget!
It's Mr. Fisk's turn to pick up his kids from school. _____ !

MAY AND MIGHT

Presentation

Modals: *May* and *Might*

Modal verbs are different from regular verbs:

- They have only one form, without *–s* or *–ed*.
- They are followed by the base form of the verb.

The modals *may* and *might* are used to talk about future possibilities.

- *May* and *might* are similar in meaning.
- To form the negative, use **may not / might not + base form** of the verb. Do not contract the negative forms *may not* and *might not*.

Notice the difference between **may be** and **maybe**. Both forms express possibility, but *maybe* is not a modal. It is an adverb, and it usually comes at the beginning of the sentence.

Examples:

I may take the bus tomorrow.

Maybe I'll take the bus tomorrow.

Incorrect: I maybe take the bus tomorrow.

Forms	Examples
may, might	It **might** rain this afternoon.
	I **may** go to a movie tonight.
may not, might not	George **may not** graduate this semester.
	Hannah **might not** want to go.

Practice 1

Circle the letter of the correct answer to complete each sentence.

Example:

1 I _____ shopping this afternoon.

   a *might to go*

   (b) *may go*

2 I'm very hungry. I _____ a steak.

   a might order

   b might to order

3 Kate _____ the meeting.

   a might attend not

   b might not attend

4 Jane _____ to bed early tonight.

   a may goes

   b may go

5 _____ Adam will come to our house for dinner on Friday.

   a May be

   b Maybe

6 It's too early to phone my sister. She _____ awake yet.

   a might not be

   b mights not be

7 Barbara _____ a blog.

   a may starts

   b might start

8 I'm tired. I _____ swimming.

   a mightn't go

   b might not go

9 **A:** Where are the children?

   B: I'm not sure.

   They _____ at the neighbor's house.

   a maybe

   b may be

10 **A:** What are you doing this afternoon?

   B: We _____ to the art museum.

   a might going

   b may go

11 Carol lost her job in Miami. She _____ to a different city.

   a may moves

   b may move

Practice 2

Complete each sentence with *may* or *might* and the verb in parentheses.

Example:

1 We *may go* (go) to Hawaii in December.

2 Jack and Jill _____ (go) to Paris for their honeymoon.

3 A: What kind of dog are you going to get?

 B: I'm not sure. We _____ (get) a poodle.

4 Helen has a fever. She _____ (not go) to her office today.

5 In five or ten years, people _____ (not use) email anymore.

6 Someday soon, we _____ (have) cars that drive themselves.

7 In the near future, paper textbooks _____ (not exist) anymore.

8 The Wilsons just had their fifth child. They _____ (need) to buy a larger house.

9 "Hello, Professor Kelly? This is Sarah Grant. You _____ (not remember) me, but I was in your Geography 103 class last semester."

10 The library is only half a mile from my house, but I _____ (drive) over there.

11 Our suitcases are too heavy. We _____ (need) to pay an excess baggage fee.

WOULD RATHER

Modals: *Would Rather*

Modal verbs are different from regular verbs:

- They have only one form, without *–s* or *–ed*.
- They are followed by the base form of the verb.

Would rather expresses preference in the present or future.

- To form affirmative sentences, use ***would rather* + base form** of the verb. *Would rather* contracts to *'d rather*.
- To form the negative, use ***would rather not* + base form** of the verb.
- To make comparisons with *would rather*, use *than*. *Than* must be followed by the base form of the verb.

Example: I'd rather watch a movie at home **than *go*** out to the movies.

Forms	Examples	Meanings
Affirmative	I **would rather** / I'**d rather** walk than drive to the theater.	I prefer to walk.
	I **would rather** / I'**d rather** walk.	
Negative	I **would rather** / I'**d rather** not eat here.	I prefer not to eat here. (I don't want to eat here.)
Yes/No questions	**Would** you **rather** walk or drive to the theater?	Do you prefer to walk or drive?
Wh- questions	What **would** you **rather** have, fish or meat?	Do you want fish or meat?

Practice 1

Circle the letter(s) of the words or phrases that correctly complete each sentence.

Example:

1 I _____ a movie _____ a book.
   a *would rather to watch*
   b *would rather watching*
   c *would rather watch*
   d *then read*
   e *then to read*
   f *than read*

2 A: Would you like to sit down?

   B: _____ , thank you.

   a I'd rather stand

   b I'd rather to stand

   c I'd rather standing

3 A: Nina is going to have a baby.

   B: Wonderful! _____ a boy or a girl?

   a Would she rather has

   b She would rather have

   c Would she rather have

4 Yanos _____ his car to work because it's difficult to find parking downtown.

   a rather would not drive

   b rather not drive

   c would rather not drive

5 After graduation, Rana _____ an apartment _____ in with her parents.

   a would rather find

   b would rather to find

   c would rather finds

   d than to move

   e than move

   f than moving

6 A: Are you married or single?

   B: _____ that question.

   a I'd rather not answer

   b I'd rather not to answer

   c I rather not answer

7 John wants to go to Canada on vacation, but his wife _____ to Mexico.

   a would rather goes

   b would rather go

   c rather go

8 Melissa _____ on a cruise _____ her family in Vermont.

   a would rather go

   b would rather to go

   c would rather going

   d than visit

   e than visiting

   f than to visit

9 Which _____ , a horror film or a comedy?

    a you would rather see

    b would you rather see

    c would rather you see

10 Gerta's parents want her to be a lawyer, but _____ a painter.

    a she'd rather be

    b she'd rather being

    c she'd rather been

11 When you fly, _____ an aisle seat or a window seat?

    a would rather you have

    b you would rather have

    c would you rather have

Practice 2

Complete each sentence with the correct form of *would rather* and the words in parentheses.

Example:

1 Gerald *would rather play* (play) guitar than *sing* (sing).

2 Josie _____ (walk) than _____ (drive) to the store.

3 _____ (you, study) at home or _____ (go) to the library?

4 A: Do you want to take the kids to the park?

    B: OK, but actually, I _____ (take) them to the zoo.

5 A: Sergio, _____ (you, buy) a laptop or a tablet computer?

    B: I _____ (buy) a laptop.

6 Mika _____ (make) dinner than _____ (eat) in a restaurant.

7 Joyce _____ (work) outdoors than _____ (sit) in an office all day.

8 A: Would you and your husband prefer a cat or a dog?

    B: Well, we _____ (get) a cat, but our son is allergic.

9 A: Do you plan to stay with your sister?

    B: Yes, but to tell you the truth, I _____ (stay) in a hotel. It's quieter.

10 Donna _____ (send) a text message than _____ (phone) her friends.

11 It's hot today. She _____ (not sit) in the sun.

Nouns

COUNT AND NONCOUNT NOUNS

Presentation

Count and Noncount Nouns

There are two types of common nouns in English: count and noncount.

Count nouns are separate things and can be counted.

- They can be singular or plural.
- They take singular or plural verbs.
- You can use the articles *a*, *an*, or *the* before count nouns.
- Plural nouns usually end with –*s*. There are some irregular plurals, for example *men*, *women*, *people*, and *children*.

Noncount nouns are not separate things and cannot be counted.

- They do not have a plural form.
- They take singular verbs.
- They are usually not written with *a* or *an*.
- You can use *some* with noncount nouns.

Forms	Examples
Singular count nouns	(a) cup, (an) apple, (a) star
Plural count nouns	cups, apples, stars
Noncount nouns	water, rice, air

Practice 1

Circle the 15 count nouns.

1 I bought a chicken and some milk at the supermarket.

2 All plants and animals require oxygen for life.

3 Many people believe that love is blind.

4 If homework is too difficult, students may feel discouraged.

5 Paul went shopping and bought two new shirts, a hat, and some paint.

6 These suitcases are too small. We need to buy new luggage.

7 Sherry loves music. She learned a new song yesterday.

8 The roses in the garden need water twice a week.

9 A poodle is a dog with short, curly hair.

Practice 2

Circle the correct noncount noun in each sentence.

Example:

1 *I bought ((some milk)/ an apple) at the supermarket.*

2 (Gas / A car) is very expensive these days.

3 Ms. Ang is worried about (money / a recession).

4 Would you like to by some (flowers / chocolate)?

5 The customers are waiting for their (water / drinks).

6 Look! We got (a package / some mail).

7 When you use a computer, be careful about (privacy / viruses).

8 Poor Mrs. Allen has (rheumatism / a headache).

9 Could you please give me (some help / a towel)?

10 The restaurant needs to get some more (waiters / furniture).

11 Sally gets nervous when she has (homework / a test).

ARTICLES A, AN, AND THE

Presentation

Articles *A, An,* and *The*

Articles come before nouns. *A* and *an* are indefinite articles. *The* is a definite article.

* Use *a/an* with singular count nouns only. Use *an* if the following noun starts with a vowel sound.

Examples: a truck, an orange

* Place *a/an* before adjectives that modify nouns. Use *an* if the adjective that modifies the noun starts with a vowel sound.

Examples: a great idea, an excellent solution

* Use *the* with singular count nouns, plural count nouns, and noncount nouns.

Examples: the boy, the trees, the air

Rules	Examples
Use *a* and *an* for a person, thing, or place that is not known or specific.	Let's go to **a restaurant**. (We don't know which restaurant.)
	Would you like **an apple**? (I don't know which apple.)
Use *a* and *an* to say what someone or something is.	I'm **a student**.
	She's **an astronaut**.
Use *the* for nouns that are used for the second time.	Yesterday I bought a car. **The car** has a sun roof. **The sun roof** needs repair.
Use *the* for people, places, or things that are unique. (There is only one.)	We had a meeting with **the president**.
	The moon is bright tonight.
Use *the* for nouns that are known to both the speaker and the listener.	I'm going to **the bank** at **the corner** of First and Main streets.
Use *the* for superlatives.	Greg is **the tallest boy** in the class.
Use *the* for nouns with modifiers (e.g., adjectives, prepositional phrases, adjective clauses).	**The milk** that I just bought is sour.
	The house on the corner is for sale.
	The black dog belongs to Marcia.
Use *the* for some names.	the United States, the Statue of Liberty, the Middle East
Do not use articles with plural count nouns and noncount nouns that are indefinite. Use *some* instead.	There are keys on the table. Are they yours?
	I bought **some milk**. We were out.
Do not use articles with plural count nouns and noncount nouns when you want to say what they are.	A: What are these? B: They're nuts. I'm baking a cake with them.
	A: What's this? B: It's chocolate milk. Would you like some?
Do not use articles to make general statements when you use plural count nouns and noncount nouns.	I love comedies.
	I enjoy music.

Practice 1

Write in the correct article to complete the paragraphs. Use *X* if you don't need an article.

a	an	the	some

Example:

1 *I had __a__ sandwich for lunch.*

2 You do not need _____ car to get around in New York City. _____ city has _____ excellent system of _____ subways and trains. In Manhattan, _____ people get around either on foot or by taxi. To catch _____ taxi, just stand in the street and stretch out your arm when _____ cab approaches.

3 American citizens need _____ passport to travel overseas. Many Asian countries and most of the countries in _____ Middle East also require you to get _____ visa. If you want to drive overseas, you might also need to get _____ international driver's license.

4 The Library of Congress in Washington, D.C., is _____ national library of _____ United States. _____ library contains _____ copy of every book sold in _____ country. There are also collections of _____ musical instruments, _____ audio recordings, _____ maps, and _____ photographs. One of the most famous documents is _____ draft of _____ speech by Abraham Lincoln.

Practice 2

Complete the sentence with *a, an,* or *the.*

Example:

1 *I ordered __a__ book from __the__ library.*

2 _____ drunk driver hit my car while I was stopped for _____ red light. I was not hurt, but _____ car was badly damaged.

3 Sarah asked her parents to give her _____ cell phone for her 12th birthday.

4 My friend and I agreed to meet at _____ library after dinner.

5 _____ tallest building in _____ world is in Dubai, United Arab Emirates.

6 Fiat is _____ car company. It is _____ largest car company in Italy.

7 _____ shoes that I bought last week are too small. I'm going to take them back to _____ store where I bought them.

8 Our air conditioner stopped working. Today _____ repairman is going to come fix it. He will need _____ ladder because it is on _____ roof.

9 My children do not like _____ pizza at Roberto's Pizzeria.

Prepositions

PREPOSITIONS OF TIME

> **Presentation**
>
> **Prepositions of Time**
>
> Prepositions link nouns, pronouns, and phrases to other words in a sentence.
>
> Prepositions of time tell us *when* something happens. The most common prepositions of time include *in*, *on*, *at*, and *from . . . to*.
>
> | Rules | | Examples |
> |---|---|---|
> | Use *in* with | parts of the day* | in the morning, in the evening |
> | | months | in December |
> | | years | in 1975 |
> | | seasons | in the summer |
> | Use *on* with | days of the week | on Tuesday |
> | | specific dates | on November 13th |
> | | holidays | on Thanksgiving |
> | | special days | on my birthday |
> | Use *at* with | specific times | at 3 o'clock
at 6 p.m.
at noon
at midnight |
> | Use *from . . . to* with | a span of time | from 2 to 4 a.m.
from Monday to Friday
from January to June |
> | *Exception: at night* | | |

Practice 1

Circle the correct preposition of time.

1 This morning I woke up (in / on / at) 7:30 a.m.

2 Mr. Cogan is a writer. He also takes care of his children. He writes (from / in / at) 8:00 (to / in / on) 12:00 every day. Then he picks up his daughter. He takes care of her (on / in / from) the afternoon.

3 Mr. Nagley is a teacher. He teaches (in / at / from) September (to / in / at) June. (At / From / In) the summer, he travels and does volunteer work.

4 My friend Stuart was born (on / in / at) December 31. In other words, he was born (in / on / at) New Year's Eve. Naturally he has a big party every year (in / at / on) his birthday!

5 I am expecting an important phone call (in / to / at) 1:00 p.m. I can meet you later (on / in / at) the afternoon.

Practice 2

Complete the sentence using *in, on, at,* or *from . . . to.*

Example:

1 *I can meet you* <u>at</u> *3:30* <u>on</u> *Thursday.*

2 I'm going to go to the gym _____ the evening.

3 **A:** Where are you going for the holidays?

   B: _____ Christmas day we're going to be with my parents.

4 Ali gets up _____ 5:00 and goes jogging.

5 Gina lived in Italy _____ 2005 _____ 2008.

6 We always go out to dinner _____ Friday nights.

7 _____ winter there are only six hours of daylight.

8 Would you like to come for a visit _____ June?

9 Let's meet for coffee _____ 4 o'clock.

10 We'll be in New York _____ May 2nd _____ the 4th.

11 Thanksgiving is always _____ the fourth Thursday _____ November.

PREPOSITIONS OF PLACE

Presentation

Prepositions of Place

Prepositions of place tell us where something is located. English has many prepositions of place. Some of the most common ones are listed in the chart.

Here is an illustration of a man's office. Look at the list of prepositions in the chart and read the examples.

Prepositions of Place	Examples
above	There's a window **above** the sofa.
across from	There is a sofa **across from** the desk.
beside, next to	There's a plant **beside / next to** the desk.
between	There's a sofa **between** the file cabinets.
in front of	There's a chair **in front of** the desk.
in the middle of	There's a rug **in the middle of** the room.
in, inside	There are documents **in / inside** the file cabinets.
on	There are papers **on** the desk.
on both sides of	There are file cabinets **on both sides of** the sofa.
on the (your) right, on the (your) left	When you enter the room, the sofa is **on the right**. The desk is **on the left**.
on top of	There's a computer **on top of** the desk.
outside	There are trees **outside** the house.
over	There are windows **over** the sofa.
under	The sofa is **under** the windows.

Practice 1

Look at the map of the college campus. Circle the letter of the correct preposition.

Example:

1 *The Fine Arts building is ___ Olive St.*

   (**a**) *on*

   b *in*

   c *between*

2 The Psychology building is _____ the History building and the graduate dormitory.

   a next to

   b between

   c in the middle of

3 The cafeteria is _____ the Administration building.

   a next to

   b across from

   c outside

4 There's a fountain _____ Adams Plaza.

   a across from

   b on top of

   c in the middle of

5 There are parking lots _____ Olive St.

   a in front of

   b on both sides of

   c under

6 The pool is _____ the gym.

   a next to

   b in

   c between

7 There are picnic tables _____ of the cafeteria.

   a outside

   b inside

   c in the middle

8 You're in the rose garden. The Fine Arts building is _____ you.

   a on top of

   b in front of

   c outside

9 The Humanities building is _____ India Road.

   a in

   b inside

   c on

10 The Physics building is _____ Adams Plaza.

   a beside

   b on

   c on both sides of

11 You are at the picnic tables. The swimming pool is _____ .

   a on your right

   b in front of the gym

   c next to the Botanical Garden

Practice 2

Look at the map of the college campus. Circle the letter of the correct preposition.

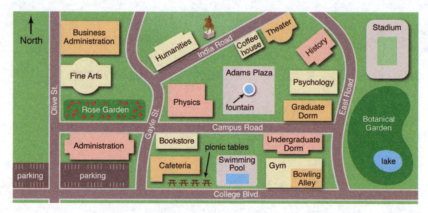

Example:

1 *The undergraduate dormitory is _____ the gym.*

   a *behind*

   b *next to*

   c *in front of*

2 The bookstore is _____ the Administration building.

   a between

   b across the street from

   c on the left of

3 There's a small lake _____ the Botanical Garden.

   a in front of

   b behind

   c in the middle of

4 You are at the intersection of Gayle St. and India Road. The Physics building is

_____ .

   a across the street

   b on your right

   c on both sides

5 There is a sculpture _____ the Humanities building.

   a next to

   b inside

   c between

6 On Campus Road, there are dormitories _____ the street.

   a on both sides of

   b across

   c behind

7 You're walking on India Road from the theater to the Humanities building. The coffee house is _____ .

   a behind you

   b on the right

   c on the left

8 The coffee house is _____ the theatre.

   a next to

   b between

   c in front of

PREPOSITIONAL PHRASES

Presentation

Prepositional Phrases

A **prepositional phrase** is a preposition followed by a noun or a noun phrase.

Examples: *to the store, with my cousin, under the table*

Prepositional phrases can express many meanings. Some common meanings are time, location, possession, direction, and description.

Meanings	Prepositions	Examples
Time	before, after, in, on, at	before dinner, after graduation, in the afternoon, on my birthday
Place	in, on, at, under, above, behind, next to, between	in the box, under the sofa, at the drugstore, between the trees, on the floor
Direction	to	to the door
Possession	of	(the owner) of the house
Description	with, from, in	the girl with the red hair, the man in the black suit, the student from Guatemala

Practice 1

Circle the letter of the prepositional phrase that completes each sentence.

Example:

1 *Christmas is always* _____ .
   (a) *on December 25*
   b *a family day*
   c *snowy and cold*

2 Cecelia usually plays tennis _____ .
   a badly
   b once a week
   c after dinner

3 The dog's favorite toy is _____ .

   a old and dirty

   b under the table

   c outside

4 I'll go _____ .

   a to the store

   b shopping

   c out later

5 The owner _____ is Mr. Agassi.

   a that we met

   b of the company

   c and manager

6 Who owns the car _____ ?

   a with the sunroof

   b that was in an accident

   c you like

7 I don't enjoy eating fruit _____ .

   a with seeds

   b that is too soft

   c every day

8 My school class has two teachers _____ .

   a who always work together

   b from Kazakhstan

   c and 35 students

9 The swimming pool will stay open _____ .

   a if the city has enough money

   b every day

   c in the winter

10 I think it's fun to drive _____ .

   a to the lake

   b very fast

   c and enjoy the view

11 Everybody listened carefully to the woman _____ .

   a who was giving instructions

   b wearing a red hat

   c in the army uniform

Practice 2

Underline the 14 prepositional phrases.

1 Every morning Robert walks to the corner and buys a newspaper.

2 My dog is an excellent guard dog. Every time the doorbell rings, he runs to the door and begins barking loudly. People who hear him think he's big and mean. But actually, he's just a cute little poodle with curly hair and a loud bark.

3 My favorite place in my grandparents' house is the front porch. I love sitting there and looking at the street. I often see the owner of the house next door working in her garden.

4 **A:** Have you ever met my boss?
B: Is he the guy in the gray suit?
C: No, that's my brother. My boss is the woman who's wearing glasses.

5 Our living room is a mess. There are old newspapers under the sofa and toys on the floor. The kids left empty soda cans everywhere. My parents are coming over after dinner. We have to clean up before they arrive!

6 I borrowed a great book from my friend. I am going to bring it with me when I go to the beach this summer.

Present

THE SIMPLE PRESENT

Presentation

The Simple Present

Use the simple present to talk about habits or customs, facts, ownership, or opinions in the present.

Examples:

I always **wash** my hands before I **eat.** (habit)

Katya **doesn't eat** meat. (habit)

Many birds **fly** south for the winter. (fact)

Penguins **don't fly.** (fact)

My house **has** a formal dining room. (ownership)

Jim **doesn't have** a big house. (ownership)

I **think** television commercials are annoying. (opinion)

Keyvan **doesn't like** tea. (opinion)

For pronouns *I, you, we,* and *they,* use the base form of the verb. Use *do not / don't* + the base form of the verb for negative statements.

For subjects in third person singular (pronouns *he, she,* and *it*), add *–s* to the verb. Use *does not / doesn't* + the base form of the verb for negative statements.

To form questions, use *do / does* + subject + base form of the verb.

The verbs *be* and *have* are irregular. *Be* is irregular in all forms. The irregular third person singular form of *have* is *has*.

Verbs	Affirmative	Negative
be (uncontracted)	I am	I am not
	you are	you are not
	he, she, it is	he, she, it is not
	we, you, they are	we, you, they are not
be (contracted)	I'm	I'm not
	you're	you're not / you aren't
	he's, she's, it's	he's not / he isn't, she's not / she isn't, it's not / it isn't
	we're, you're, they're	we're not / we aren't, you're not / you aren't, they're not / they aren't
Other verbs	I / You / We / They dance.	I / You / We / They do not (don't) dance.
	He / She / It dances.	He / She / It does not (doesn't) dance.

Practice 1

Circle the letter of the correct form of the verb to complete each sentence.

Example:

1 *Thailand* _____ *four seasons.*
  a *not have*
  b *don't have*
  ⓒ *doesn't have*

2 In tropical countries, it _____ every afternoon.
  a rain
  b rains
  c raining

3 Joyce _____ happy with the color of her new car.
  a isn't
  b be
  c aren't

4 Every culture _____ unique rules for correct behavior.

    a have

    b has

    c having

5 If someone invites you to dinner at their home, it _____ polite to bring a gift.

    a be

    b is

    c are

6 Americans usually _____ gifts in business situations.

    a not give

    b doesn't give

    c don't give

7 In most cultures, people _____ when they are happy.

    a smiles

    b smile

    c smiled

8 Sonya _____ a car.

    a doesn't have

    b don't have

    c not have

9 No one is answering the phone at my parents' house. They _____ home.

    a not

    b aren't

    c isn't

10 Peter _____ most reality television shows are silly.

    a thinks

    b think

    c thinking

11 After college, Sue and Sally _____ to live with their parents.

    a not want

    b doesn't want

    c don't want

Practice 2

Complete each sentence with the correct simple present form of the verb in parentheses.

Example:

1 *I <u>do not like</u> (not like) very salty food.*

2 The U.S. flag _____ (have) 13 stripes and 50 stars.

3 You _____ (not need) to attend the meeting.

4 The lights _____ (be) on in my neighbors' house, but the neighbors _____ (not be) home.

5 Jacob and Mary _____ (not want) to get married in a church. They _____ (prefer) a nontraditional wedding.

6 I _____ (has) a very quiet dog. He _____ (not bark) very often.

7 My hamster _____ (eat) five times a day. Before eating, she always _____ (play) on her wheel.

8 My friend Jackson _____ (be) a vegetarian. He _____ (not eat) meat.

9 We _____ (live) in an apartment. We _____ (not have) our own parking space.

10 My roommate Mark _____ (speak) Japanese, but he _____ (not be) from Japan.

11 The car _____ (not have) enough room for six passengers.

THE PRESENT PROGRESSIVE

The Present Progressive

Use the present progressive to talk about things that are happening now. The form of the present progressive is **be (not)** + **verb** + **-ing**.

Forms	Affirmative	Negative
Singular	I am / I'm eating.	I am not / I'm not working.
	You are / You're eating.	You are not / You're not / You aren't working.
	He is / He's eating.	He is not / He's not / He isn't working.
	She is / She's eating.	She is not / She's not / She isn't working.
	It is / It's eating.	It is not / It's not / It isn't working.
Plural	We are / We're eating.	We are not / We aren't / We're not working.
	They are / They're eating.	They are not / They aren't / They're not working.

Rules	Examples
You can use the present progressive with these time expressions: *right now, at this moment, today, these days, this morning/afternoon/after, this week/month/year.*	Jun **is studying** in Texas these days.
	Right now the teacher **is correcting** papers. She **isn't planning** lessons.
Do not use the present progressive to talk about habits or facts that do not change. Use the simple present.	<u>Correct:</u> Alberto **swims** every day. <u>Incorrect:</u> Alberto is swimming every day.
We usually do not use the present progressive with non-action verbs such as *have, be, look, want, believe, know, need, hear, see, like, love,* and *think.* We use the simple present.	<u>Correct:</u> I **want** a cup of coffee. <u>Incorrect:</u> I am wanting a cup of coffee.
Some non-action verbs can take the present progressive, but the meaning is different. Some of these verbs include *have* (= "eat" or "drink"), *think* (= "using my mind"), *love* (= "enjoy"), *see* (= "date").	I **have** two cats. *(non-action)* I'**m having** dinner right now. *(action)*
	I **think** you're wonderful. *(non-action)* I'**m thinking** about my brother. *(action)*
	I **love** my sister. *(non-action)* I'**m loving** this weather. *(action)*
	I **see** Dana. *(non-action)* I'**m seeing** Dana. *(action)*

Practice 1

Underline the correct verb form that correctly completes each sentence.

Example:

1 I (<u>want</u> / am wanting) a cup of coffee right now.

2 I (am not needing / don't need) any help right now, thanks.

3 **A:** Hello, is Andrea home?
   B: No. She (walks / is walking) the dog at the moment.

4 **A:** What's that noise?
   B: What noise? I (am not hearing / don't hear) anything.

5 I (don't believe / am not believing) in superstitions.

6 Fifty people (stand / are standing) in line to get into the nightclub.

7 You (are looking / look) fantastic. I (am loving / love) your new hairstyle.

8 Can you hear? The neighbors (have / are having) the same argument again.

9 **A:** Hey, are you OK? You (are seeming / seem) sad.
   B: I ('m thinking / think) about my aunt. She's sick.

10 **A:** What (do you look / are you looking) at?
   B: There! I ('m thinking / think) it's a whale.
   A: Where? I ('m not seeing / don't see) anything.

11 Franco (doesn't have / is not having) dinner now. He ('s sleeping / sleeps).

Practice 2

Complete each sentence with the simple present or present progressive form of the verb in parentheses.

Example:

1 Jim <u>'s washing</u> (wash) his car right now.

2 You _____ (do) it wrong. Let me help you.

3 Please don't go in the baby's room. She _____ (sleep).

4 The buses _____ (not run) today, so we have to stay home.

5 I'm sorry you _____ (not feel) well at the moment.

6 This semester I _____ (take) four classes.

7 The washing machine _____ (not work). I'm going to call a repairman.

8 **A:** Did you hear about Rick and Anna? They _____ (see) each other.
   B: That's great! I _____ (think) they're perfect for each other.

9 You can borrow our car. We _____ (not use) it today.

Past

THE SIMPLE PAST

Presentation

The Simple Past

Use the simple past to write about events that began and ended in the past. To form the simple past, add *–ed* to the base form of the verb.

Rules	Examples
The regular past has three spellings. For most verbs, add -*ed* to the base form.	I **waited** for two hours.
If a verb ends in *e*, add -*d*.	They **lived** in Berlin.
If a verb ends in *y*, then drop the *y* and add -*ied*. There are some exceptions: stay > stayed, enjoy > enjoyed, play > played	She **studied** for six hours.
All subjects have the same form.	I / You / He / We / They **enjoyed** the show.
Use *did not (didn't)* for the negative. Do not add -*ed* to the base form. All subjects have the same form.	I / You / She / We / They **did not / didn't finish**.
To form questions, use *did* + subject + base form of the verb.	**Did you go** to Italy last year?
Be is irregular in the past.	I / He / She / It **was** happy.
	We / You / They **were** late.
Many other verbs have irregular past forms. Some of these verbs include: buy > bought, eat > ate, drink > drank, go > went, have > had, hear > heard, leave > left, put > put, ride > rode, run > ran, say > said, see > saw, sit > sat	We **saw** a movie last night.
	We **didn't buy** popcorn.

Practice 1

Complete each sentence with the past form of the verb in parentheses.

Example:

1 *Yesterday we* <u>walked</u> *(walk) from our house to the beach.*

2 On the way we _____ (decide) to stop at a coffee shop.

3 We _____ (not hurry).

4 We _____ (stay) there for about 30 minutes.

5 Then we _____ (continue) on our walk.

6 We _____ (arrive) at the beach just before sunset.

7 We _____ (not have) a blanket, so we _____ (sit) on the sand.

8 We _____ (watch) the sun go down.

9 We _____ (enjoy) the sunset.

10 We _____ (leave) before dark.

11 We _____ (not want) to walk home, so we _____ (call) a taxi.

Practice 2

Complete each sentence with the past form of the verb in parentheses.

Example:

1 *Yesterday we* <u>walked</u> *(walk) from our house to the beach.*

2 July was a bad month for fires in California. There _____ (be) more than 50 fires between July 1 and July 31. The fires _____ (cause) several injuries and _____ (leave) a lot of destruction in some of the mountain areas. People also _____ (report) fires in San Diego, Los Angeles, and Santa Barbara counties. Many fires _____ (happen) near populated areas.

News reports _____ (warn) people to get out of the dangerous areas. Many people _____ (hear) the warnings. Still, some people _____ (not believe) the reports. They _____ (not leave). This _____ (be) a mistake. The fires _____ (arrive) suddenly. They _____ (kill) two people and _____ (injure) 25, including a dozen fire fighters.

3 My friend Donna _____ (celebrate) her 30th birthday with a trip to Russia and parts of Asia. She _____ (go) by herself. She _____ (visit) many amazing countries including Azerbaijan, Kazakhstan, and Mongolia. She _____ (stay) in Mongolia for two weeks. She _____ (meet) many great people, and she _____ (try) a lot of delicious food. She _____ (want) to stay longer, but she _____ (not have) any more time or money.

THE PAST PROGRESSIVE

Presentation

The Past Progressive

To form the past progressive, use:

I / he / she / it **was (not)** + verb + **-ing**

Examples: I was sleeping.

Joe wasn't eating dinner.

you / we / they **were (not)** + verb + **-ing**

Examples: We were watching TV.

You weren't listening.

Use the past progressive in these situations:

Rules	Examples
To describe an event that was happening at a specific time in the past.	At 9 p.m., they **were watching** TV.
To describe a past event that was happening when another event interrupted it.	I **was washing** the dishes when the phone rang.

Practice 1

Circle the letter of the correct form of the past progressive.

Example:

1 *At 9 o'clock last night, Ali* _____.

  a *studying*

  ⓑ *was studying*

  c *were studying*

2 At noon yesterday, everyone in the Floren family was out. The kids were at school. They _____ lunch.

  a was eating

  b eating

  c were eating

3 Mrs. Floren was at work. She _____ to a client on the phone.

  a talking

  b was talking

  c were talking

4 Mr. Floren _____ to the airport to pick up one of his colleagues.

   a were driving
   b was driving
   c driving

5 Only the dog and the cat were at home. They _____.

   a sleep
   b was sleeping
   c were sleeping

6 It was a typical Saturday morning at the park. Some children _____ in the sandbox.

   a digging
   b were digging
   c was digging

7 A couple of old men _____ a game of chess.

   a playing
   b were playing
   c was playing

8 A jogger _____ around the park.

   a was running
   b were running
   c running

9 A woman _____ on a bench. She _____ a newspaper.

   a sit
   b was sitting
   c sitting
   d read
   e was reading
   f were reading

10 Two friends _____ on the grass.

   a lying
   b were lying
   c was lying

11 People of all ages _____ the beautiful sunny day.

   a enjoy
   b were enjoying
   c was enjoying

Practice 2

Complete each sentence with the past progressive form of the verb in parentheses.

Example:

1 *Mr. Adams was not home last week. He <u>was working</u> (work) out of town.*

2 Last night I had a strange dream. In my dream it was 2 a.m. I _____ (walk) down the street. All my neighbors _____ (sleep). It was perfectly quiet. It _____ (not snow). Suddenly I saw an elephant. It _____ (stand) next to my car. I walked over and I asked the elephant, "Why are you here?" The elephant answered, "I _____ (wait) for you. Can you take me to the airport?"

3 This morning, I was on an elevator with seven or eight other people. It was interesting to watch them. One guy _____ (listen) to music. Two people _____ (read) the newspaper. One woman _____ (talk) on the phone. Another guy _____ (eat) a muffin. The rest of us _____ (not do) anything special.

SENTENCE STRUCTURE

Simple Sentences

SUBJECT/VERB COMBINATIONS

Presentation

Subject/Verb Combinations

A sentence is a group of words with a subject and a verb.

- A simple sentence has one subject + verb combination.
- Both the subject and the verb can be "compound." That is, they can include more than one noun or verb.

Patterns	Examples
one noun + one verb	The **students entered** the room.
two or more nouns + one verb	The **students** and the **teacher entered** the room.
one noun + two or more verbs	The **students entered** the room and **sat** down.
Two or more nouns + two or more verbs	The **students** and the **teacher entered** the room and **sat** down.

Practice 1

Circle the letter of the correct pattern for each sentence.

Example:

1 *Sandra and Ellen live in a dormitory.*
  a *one noun + one verb*   **c** *two nouns + one verb*
  b *one noun + two verbs*   **d** *two nouns + two verbs*

2 People climb Mount Everest every year.
  a one noun + one verb   **c** two nouns + one verb
  b one noun + two verbs   **d** two nouns + two verbs

3 The United States and Canada share a border.
  a one noun + one verb   **c** two nouns + one verb
  b one noun + two verbs   **d** two nouns + two verbs

4 The singers and the musicians returned to the stage and bowed.

  a one noun + one verb   **c** two nouns + one verb

  b one noun + two verbs   **d** two nouns + two verbs

5 Sharon came home and immediately checked her email.

  a one noun + one verb   **c** two nouns + one verb

  b one noun + two verbs   **d** two nouns + two verbs

6 Tom and Linda are meeting us for coffee.

  a one noun + one verb   **c** two nouns + one verb

  b one noun + two verbs   **d** two nouns + two verbs

7 The cat refused the food.

  a one noun + one verb   **c** two nouns + one verb

  b one noun + two verbs   **d** two nouns + two verbs

8 My best friend and I talk or text every day.

  a one noun + one verb   **c** two nouns + one verb

  b one noun + two verbs   **d** two nouns + two verbs

9 The gardener will cut the grass and water the flowers.

  a one noun + one verb   **c** two nouns + one verb

  b one noun + two verbs   **d** two nouns + two verbs

10 We fly to San Francisco on Friday and return on Sunday.

  a one noun + one verb   **c** two nouns + one verb

  b one noun + two verbs   **d** two nouns + two verbs

11 Karen and Cynthia work in the same office and share an apartment.

  a one noun + one verb   **c** two nouns + one verb

  b one noun + two verbs   **d** two nouns + two verbs

Practice 2

Write the subject and the verb of each sentence. Include *and* for compound subjects or verbs.

Example:

1 *My cousins and I went to the football game on Friday night.*

  Subject: <u>cousins and I</u>

  Verb: <u>went</u>

2 The fox jumped over the fence and disappeared.

  Subject: _____

  Verb: _____

3 Dave awoke and took a shower.

Subject: _____

Verb: _____

4 Silvio is from Romania and speaks Romanian.

Subject: _____

Verb: _____

5 Sam and Roger had an argument.

Subject: _____

Verb: _____

6 At the end of the day, my wife and I are tired.

Subject: _____

Verb: _____

7 Mary forgot her bag at school.

Subject: _____

Verb: _____

8 Fernanda and Carlos are from Spain.

Subject: _____

Verb: _____

9 Aziz bought a new computer and monitor.

Subject: _____

Verb: _____

10 My brother and sister graduated from college and moved to New York.

Subject: _____

Verb: _____

11 The wedding started at 5 p.m. and ended at 11 p.m.

Subject: _____

Verb: _____

CONJUNCTIONS AND AND OR

Copyright © 2017 by Pearson Education, Inc. Duplication is not permitted.

Presentation

Conjunctions *And* and *Or*

Words that connect words or groups of words in a sentence are called *conjunctions*. Two of the most common conjunctions are *and* and *or*. They have different meanings.

Rules	Examples
Use *and* to connect subjects or objects in an affirmative sentence. Use a plural verb when you connect subjects.	Coffee **and** tea are the most popular hot drinks in North America. *(connecting subjects)*
	Janice can speak English, Spanish, **and** German. *(connecting objects)*
Use *or* to connect objects in a negative sentence	Tony doesn't eat meat **or** fish.
	Carla doesn't have a car **or** a bicycle.
Use *or* to connect choices (subjects or objects)	Ken **or** Irene will cook dinner tonight. *(connecting subjects)*
	Did they buy a Honda **or** a Toyota? *(connecting objects)*

Practice 1

Write the two sentences as one sentence using *and* or *or*. Change the verb form if necessary.

Example:

1 *I.M. Pei is a famous architect. Antoni Gaudi is a famous architect.*
   I.M. Pei and Antoni Gaudi are famous architects .

2 I like strawberries. I like bananas.

   _____

3 Ellen will take the bus to the party. Jake will take the bus to the party.

   _____

4 I can't speak German. I can't speak Russian.

   _____

5 Susan will graduate in 2018. David will graduate in 2018.

_____

6 Do you own a car? Do you own a motorcycle?

_____

7 New York City has a lot of people. Los Angeles has a lot of people.

_____

8 Tom Cruise will get the star role in the new action film. Daniel Craig will get the star role in the new action film.

_____

9 Would you like chocolate cake for dessert? Would you like apple pie for dessert?

_____

10 Please give me the hammer. Please give me the nails.

_____

11 The country doesn't have mountains. The country doesn't have lakes.

_____

Practice 2

Write in the correct conjunction to complete each sentence.

Example:

1 _The package will arrive tomorrow <u>or</u> the next day._

2 I don't like very hot weather _____ very cold weather.

3 My family has two cats, two dogs, _____ three birds.

4 **A:** Who is going to host the 2018 Winter Olympics?
B: South Korea _____ Canada—I can't remember.

5 **A:** Would you like hamburgers _____ pizza for dinner?
B: I'd like hamburgers.

6 Apples, oranges, _____ peaches have a lot of vitamin C.

7 Skunks _____ stink bugs are animals that use a bad smell to protect themselves.

8 The apartment doesn't have a washing machine _____ a dryer.

9 A: What did you have for breakfast this morning?

  B: I had a glass of orange juice _____ toast.

10 Ms. Andrews _____ Mr. Baker will be the new business
manager.

11 My daughter doesn't like milk _____ eggs.

Compound Sentences

COORDINATING CONJUNCTIONS AND, BUT, OR, AND SO

Presentation

Coordinating Conjunctions *And*, *But*, *Or*, and *So*

A *compound sentence* consists of two simple sentences and a connecting word, called a *coordinating conjunction*. The most common coordinating conjunctions are *and*, *but*, *or*, and *so*. A comma comes before these coordinating conjunctions in a compound sentence.

Rules	Examples
And connects two sentences with similar ideas.	Susan's dog is very intelligent, **and** he loves to play.
But connects sentences with contrasting ideas.	Peter's dog is very gentle, **but** he's not very smart.
So introduces a sentence containing a result.	My father dislikes animals, **so** I have never had a pet.
Or connects sentences that express choices or possibilities.	We may get a dog, **or** we might get another cat.

Practice 1

Circle the letter next to the correct conjunction to complete each compound sentence.

Example:

1 *George wants to make more money, _____ he is going to look for a better job.*

   a *and*   **ⓑ** *so*   **c** *but*

2 Donna has visited South America, _____ she hasn't been to Asia.

   a and   **b** but   **c** so

3 My grandfather runs a mile every day, _____ he swims three or four miles a week.

   a and   **b** but   **c** so

4 College students can live in a dormitory on campus, _____ they can rent an apartment off campus.

   a and   **b** or   **c** so

5 Steve's birthday is August 21, _____ his sister's is one day later.

   a and   **b** or   **c** so

6 I want to get more exercise, _____ I am going to start riding my bike to work.

   a and   **b** but   **c** so

7 Is your sister planning to start college, _____ will she join the military?

   a and   **b** but   **c** or

8 My sister never answers her phone, _____ she always responds to a text message.

   a and   **b** but   **c** so

9 Working on a computer can cause hand injuries, _____ remember to take breaks often.

   a but   **b** or   **c** so

10 Jack loves playing golf, _____ his wife hates it.

   a and   **b** but   **c** so

11 Switzerland has four official languages, _____ most people speak at least two of them.

   a and   **b** but   **c** so

Practice 2

Write the two sentences as one sentence using a comma + *and*, *or*, *but*, or *so*. Change the capital letter in the second sentence to lowercase.

Example:

1 *It's raining. We can't go to the park.*
   It's raining, so we can't go to the park.

2 John goes to college. He likes it. _____

3 I would love to take a Chinese class. I don't have time. _____

4 Juan might order a steak. He might get the fish. _____

5 My mother did not answer the phone. I left her a message. _____

6 My boss is an excellent manager. She is a good listener. _____

7 I wanted to sing the song. I couldn't remember the words. _____

8 The tree is dead. We have to cut it down. _____

9 Do you need to leave? Can you stay for dinner? _____

10 I can send you an email. I can call you. _____

11 John lost his textbook. He couldn't study for the test. _____

NEITHER AND NOT EITHER TO EXPRESS SIMILAR IDEAS

Presentation

Neither and *Not Either* to Express Similar Ideas

You can use *neither* or *not either* to combine two negative sentences that compare similar things.

- Use an auxiliary verb (*do*, *have*, or *be*) in the second sentence.
- Put a comma before *and*.
- The verb tenses in the two combined sentences are the same.

Rules	Examples
In a clause with *not either*, word order is subject + verb + *not either*. *Not* can form a contraction with the auxiliary verb.	Joyce isn't tall, and **Yolanda is not either**. / Joyce isn't tall, and **Yolanda isn't either**.
	Mina didn't finish the test, and **Joe did not either**. / Mina didn't finish the test, and **Joe didn't either**.
	Mike won't go to the party, and **Tom will not either**. / Mike won't go to the party, and **Tom won't either**.
In a clause with *neither*, word order is *neither* + verb + subject. The auxiliary verb that follows *neither* is affirmative.	Joyce isn't tall, and **neither is Yolanda**.
	Mina didn't finish the test, and **neither did Joe**.
	Mike won't go to the party, and **neither will Tom**.

Practice 1

Circle the letter that correctly identifies whether each sentence is correct or incorrect.

Example:

1 *Tom doesn't smoke, and Alex doesn't neither.*
   a *Correct*
   (b) *Incorrect*

2 California doesn't have a high-speed rail system, and Texas does either.
   a Correct
   b Incorrect

3 Giraffes cannot swim, and neither hippopotamuses can.
   a Correct
   b Incorrect

4 My black pants aren't clean, and my brown ones aren't either.
   a Correct
   b Incorrect

5 Jack doesn't have a smart phone, and Jennifer doesn't either.
   a Correct
   b Incorrect

6 Miki doesn't smoke, and neither Kazu.
   a Correct
   b Incorrect

7 Mark doesn't have children, and Hans doesn't either.
   a Correct
   b Incorrect

8 Joe's Market doesn't sell fruit, and Jan's Market does neither.
   a Correct
   b Incorrect

9 Kara isn't working right now, and Marvin either isn't.
   a Correct
   b Incorrect

10 The house doesn't have wireless Internet, and neither the restaurant does.
   a Correct
   b Incorrect

11 Paul didn't know the words to the song, and Martin didn't either.
   a Correct
   b Incorrect

Practice 2

Write the missing words in the correct order.

1 The dishwasher doesn't work, and _____ _____

_____ _____ .

    doesn't   either   clothes dryer   the

2 Ben can't play the guitar, and _____ _____ _____ .

    either   can't   Joan

3 The Browns don't belong to a church, and _____ _____

_____ _____ .

    Smiths   the   neither   do

4 Mr. Grippas didn't go to college, and _____ _____

_____ _____ .

    did   wife   his   neither

5 Teachers won't receive a pay increase this year, and _____ _____

_____ .

    either   won't   bus drivers

6 Ireland doesn't have any snakes, and _____ _____

_____ .

    does   New Zealand   neither

7 The soup didn't have enough salt, and _____ _____

_____ .

    either   didn't   the potatoes

8 My aunt wasn't home, and _____ _____

_____ _____ .

    neither   uncle   was   my

9 Francois didn't buy anything at the mall, and _____ _____

_____ .

    Steven   either   didn't

10 The conversation wasn't interesting, and _____ _____

_____ .

    the movie   wasn't   either

SO AND TOO TO EXPRESS SIMILAR IDEAS

Presentation

So and *Too* to Express Similar Ideas

You can use *so* and *too* to combine two affirmative sentences that compare similar things.

- Use an auxiliary verb (*do*, *have*, or *be*) in the second sentence.
- The auxiliary verb should have the same verb tense as the verb in the first sentence.
- Put a comma before *and*.

Rules	Examples
In a clause with *so*, the word order is *so* + verb + subject. The verb *be* must remain *be* in both sentences.	Marta is a dentist, and **so is Jackie**.
	David has a beautiful garden, and so **does Angela**.
	Tamara will get a promotion, and **so will Kate**.
In a clause with *too*, the word order is subject + verb + *too*. The verb *be* must remain *be* in both sentences.	Marta is a dentist, and **Jackie is too**.
	David has a beautiful garden, and **Angela does too**.
	Tamara will get a promotion, and **Kate will too**.

Practice 1

Circle the letter that correctly identifies whether each sentence is correct or incorrect.

Example:

1 *Trisha loves ice cream, and Frank too.*
  a *Correct*
  ⓑ *Incorrect*

2 France has a high-speed rail system, and Japan does so.
  a Correct
  b Incorrect

3 Costa Rica is a tropical country, and so is Thailand.
  a Correct
  b Incorrect

4 They visited the pyramids in Mexico, and so I did.
  a Correct
  b Incorrect

5 Saudi Arabia exports oil, and Egypt too.
  a Correct
  b Incorrect

6 A Porsche is an expensive European sports car, and so is a Ferrari.
  a Correct
  b Incorrect

7 Sydney, Australia, has a famous opera house, and Milan, Italy does, too.
  a Correct
  b Incorrect

8 My best friend is serving in the military, and her brother too.
  a Correct
  b Incorrect

9 A laptop computer requires a wireless connection, and a tablet computer too.
  a Correct
  b Incorrect

10 Mt. Kilimanjaro has snow all year, and so Mt. Everest.
  a Correct
  b Incorrect

11 Owls are night animals, and so are bats.
  a Correct
  b Incorrect

Practice 2

Write the missing words in the correct order.

Example:

1 *Korea exports cars, and* _____so_____ _____does_____ _____Japan_____ .
   so   does   Japan

2 My parents have a house with a swimming pool, _____
   _____ _____ _____ .
   my grandparents   too   and   do

3 "Macoun" is a variety of apple, _____ _____ _____ _____ .
   is   too   "Gala"   and

4 Rina is a vegetarian, _____ _____ _____ _____ .
   and   Michiko   so   is

5 Gloria believes in ghosts, _____ _____ _____ _____ .
   too   and   Oliver   does

6 Italian food uses a lot of garlic, _____ _____
   _____ _____ .
   so   does   and   Spanish food

7 Dolphins are not fish. They are mammals, _____ _____
   _____ _____ .
   and   so   are   whales

8 Marco will graduate from college this year, _____ _____
   _____ _____ .
   will   too   and   Sheila

9 On weekends, Greg volunteers at an animal shelter, _____ _____
   _____ _____ .
   too   Cheryl   does   and

10 New York City is a large city, _____ _____
   _____ _____ .
   is   Chicago   so   and

116   SENTENCE STRUCTURE

Complex Sentences

INDEPENDENT AND DEPENDENT CLAUSES

Presentation

Independent and Dependent Clauses

A *clause* is a group of words with a subject and a verb.

- An *independent clause* is like a simple sentence. It expresses a complete thought.

Example: *We visited the Eiffel Tower.*

- An independent clause can stand alone.
- A *dependent clause* cannot stand alone. You must connect it to an independent clause. The dependent clause can come before or after the independent clause. If it comes first, put a comma after it.

Example: *After we toured the Louvre, we visited the Eiffel Tower.*

Dependent clauses begin with words called subordinators. Subordinators can express many meanings. Some of the most common ones are time, reason, and condition.

Meaning	Subordinators	Examples
Time	before, after, when, as soon as	**After** we ate, we washed the dishes.
		Everyone stood up **as soon as** the plane landed.
Reason	because, since	**Since** it was very hot, we stayed indoors.
Condition	If	**If** the weather is nice, then we'll eat outside.

Practice 1

Are these dependent or independent clauses? Circle the letter of the correct answer.

Example:

1 *Because we didn't have any money.*
  a Dependent clause
  b Independent clause

2 Tom Cruise is a famous movie star.
   a Dependent clause
   b Independent clause

3 He was a terrible student.
   a Dependent clause
   b Independent clause

4 He has trouble reading.
   a Dependent clause
   b Independent clause

5 After Julia moved to New York.
   a Dependent clause
   b Independent clause

6 Because he has a condition called dyslexia.
   a Dependent clause
   b Independent clause

7 If you leave work early.
   a Dependent clause
   b Independent clause

8 As soon as you get off the train.
   a Dependent clause
   b Independent clause

9 I'll wait for you at the station.
   a Dependent clause
   b Independent clause

10 Because James has a high fever.
   a Dependent clause
   b Independent clause

11 When Mrs. Adams writes to her grandchildren.
   a Dependent clause
   b Independent clause

12 Since the car didn't start this morning.
   a Dependent clause
   b Independent clause

Practice 2

Underline eight dependent clauses in the activity.

Example:

<u>After the guests went home,</u> we cleaned up.

Sharon:	Jack's 21st birthday is on Saturday. We're planning a surprise party. Can you help me plan it?
Max:	Sure. What do you need?
Sharon:	Well, we need to clean the apartment, prepare food, and buy drinks. And after all the guests arrive, someone needs to bring Jack to the party.
Max:	I can do that. I'm taking Jack to dinner that night. While we're eating, the guests can come over. After we are done, I'll tell Jack to stop by your apartment because I forgot my guitar there. As soon as we arrive, everybody will shout "Surprise!"
Sharon:	That's a great plan. Now let's plan the menu. Oh, we need a cake.
Max:	I'll get it if you tell me the name of a bakery.
Sharon:	The Cake Factory is the best place. But go early in the morning if you want to find a parking place.

SUBORDINATING CONJUNCTIONS OF TEMPORALITY

Presentation

Subordinating Conjunctions of Temporality

Complex sentences have one independent clause and at least one dependent clause. An independent clause is a complete sentence. It can stand by itself. A dependent clause is not complete. It must combine with an independent clause. Dependent clauses begin with *subordinators*. If you write the dependent clause first, place a comma after it. If you write the independent clause first, don't use a comma.

Subordinators can introduce many types of clauses. Subordinators that introduce clauses about *when* something happened are called **time subordinators** and include *before, after, when, while,* and *as soon as.*

Remember:

A time clause has a subject and a verb. A prepositional phrase has only a preposition and a noun. Compare:

After I check my email (time clause)

After dinner (prepositional phrase)

Rules	Examples
Before describes an action that happens earlier than another action.	Wash your hands **before** you begin eating.
	Before you begin eating, wash your hands.
After describes an action that happens later than another action.	I'll walk the dog **after** I check my email.
	After I check my email, I'll walk the dog.
While describes two actions happening at the same time.	I like to read the newspaper **while** I eat breakfast.
	While I eat breakfast, I like to read the newspaper.
As soon as means "immediately after" or "at the moment when."	The students stopped talking **as soon as** the bell rang.
	As soon as the bell rang, the students stopped talking.
When means "at the time that" and "whenever."	**When** I arrive, I'll call you.
	The ground gets wet **when** it rains.

Practice 1

Underline the nine time clauses in the paragraph.

Anya likes to exercise after she gets up in the morning. She loves to swim. She goes swimming several times a week before work. The pool opens at 7 a.m. Anya usually arrives a few minutes early. While she's waiting, she chats with the other early swimmers. When the doors open, she enters the locker room and puts on her bathing suit. Before she enters the pool, she takes a quick shower. As soon as she enters the water, she begins swimming quickly. She usually swims for about 40 minutes. While she swims, she counts laps and daydreams. She always feels relaxed and refreshed when she gets out of the pool. After swimming, she takes a long, hot shower. Then she gets dressed for work and dries her hair. She always says good-bye to the lifeguards before she leaves the pool. When she arrives at the office, she is in a good mood.

Practice 2

Underline the correct subordinator in brackets to complete each sentence.

Paragraph 1

John and his best friend, Thomas, will both graduate from high school next spring. They plan to do different things [after, before, while] they graduate. John wants to be an engineer. He plans to start college [as soon as, while, before] he graduates. He wants to finish college quickly and start working at his father's engineering firm. Thomas, on the other hand, isn't sure what he wants to study, so he plans to join the army [before, while, as soon as] he goes to college. He thinks he can learn some useful skills [while, as soon as, after] he is a soldier. Serving in the army will also give him time to decide what he wants to study [when, before, while] he goes to college.

Paragraph 2

Nothing special happened on my flight to Seattle last week. My brother drove me to the airport. [When, Before, While] I arrived at the check-in area, I printed out my boarding pass and checked my luggage. Then I went upstairs and got in line for the security check. [While, Before, As soon as] I was waiting, I phoned my sister, and we spoke for about ten minutes. [When, While, After] it was my turn to go through the X-ray screening, I took off my shoes and my jacket and put them in a bin. I watched them disappear into the X-ray machine. Next, I took my keys out of my pocket, put them into a bowl, and walked through the metal detector. On the other side, I picked up my shoes and my jacket. After that, I started walking to my gate. I was early, so I stopped at one of the restaurants and had a sandwich. [After, While, Before] I finished eating, I paid my bill and walked to my departure gate. Passengers were already boarding the flight [when, while, after] I arrived. [As soon as, While, Before] it was my turn, I boarded the plane and found my seat. Soon we were in the air. After a comfortable and uneventful three-hour flight, I landed in Seattle.

REASON, CONDITION, AND TIME SUBORDINATORS

Presentation

Reason, Condition, and Time Subordinators

Complex sentences have one independent clause and at least one dependent clause. Dependent clauses begin with words called *subordinators*. If you write the dependent clause first, place a comma after it. If you write the independent clause first, do not use a comma.

The subordinators **because** and **since** introduce reasons. The subordinator **if** introduces a condition or conditions. **Since** can also be used as an adverb to indicate time.

Rules	Examples
In reason clauses, *because* and *since* have the same meaning. They tell you the cause for something. Don't begin a sentence with *because*.	I don't like swimming in the morning **because / since** the water is cold.
	Since the water is cold, I do not like swimming in the morning.
Since is also used in time clauses. It means "from then until now."	Sharon has played the piano **since** she was four.
	Since she was four, Sharon has played the piano.
If introduces a condition.	**If** I eat late at night, then I have trouble falling asleep.
	I have trouble falling asleep **if** I eat late at night.

Practice 1

Is this a reason, condition, or time clause? Circle the letter next to the correct answer.

1 If the car won't start, I'll take the bus to work.
   a Condition
   b Reason
   c Time

2 Please close the door if the air conditioning is on.
   a Condition
   b Reason
   c Time

3 I wasn't able to go out today because I lost my car keys.
   a Condition
   b Reason
   c Time

4 Since there was no school on Monday, the children were allowed to stay up late on Sunday.
   a Condition
   b Reason
   c Time

5 If you have a university degree in business, you can get a job in almost any kind of industry.
   a Condition
   b Reason
   c Time

6 My parents have lived in the same house since they got married.
   a Condition
   b Reason
   c Time

7 I stayed home from school since I had a bad headache.
   a Condition
   b Reason
   c Time

8 It will take Allison five years to finish college because she is both working and going to school.
   a Condition
   b Reason
   c Time

9 I admire my uncle because he is intelligent and successful.
  - **a** Condition
  - **b** Reason
  - **c** Time

10 Since we moved to this house, we have had eight dogs and cats.
  - **a** Condition
  - **b** Reason
  - **c** Time

11 The house gets very hot if all the windows are closed.
  - **a** Condition
  - **b** Reason
  - **c** Time

Practice 2

Write *because*, *since*, or *if* to complete each sentence. For some items, more than one correct answer is possible.

Example:

1 *Marilyn rarely eats dessert* <u>because / since</u> *she doesn't like sweet foods.*

2 Tourists love to visit Los Angeles, California, _____ there are many interesting things to do.

3 _____ it rains, the mushrooms will grow.

4 Most surfers wear wet suits _____ the water in the Pacific Ocean is quite cold.

5 You can participate in outdoor sports all year round _____ the weather is almost always nice.

6 The best time to swim outdoors is in the late morning or early afternoon _____ it is usually windy in the late afternoon.

7 The Johnsons have owned a condominium near the beach _____ their children were young.

8 The concert was cancelled _____ the singer had a sore throat.

9 Call me _____ you need a ride to the party.

10 _____ the United States became an independent country, it has had more than 40 presidents.

11 Jordan wants to become a veterinarian _____ he has always loved animals.

ADJECTIVE CLAUSES

Presentation

Adjective Clauses

Adjective clauses (also called **relative clauses**) are a type of dependent clause. They give information about nouns, and they come right after the nouns they modify. The nouns can be the subject, object, or object of a preposition.

Adjective clauses start with subordinators called **relative pronouns**. The three most common relative pronouns are *who*, *that*, and *which*.

There are two kinds of relative clauses: restrictive and non-restrictive. A **restrictive clause** gives necessary information about the noun. A **non-restrictive clause** gives additional or new information about the noun. Commas separate the non-restrictive clause in a sentence.

Examples:

A person who is not reliable is not a good friend. (restrictive)

Rachel, who is not reliable, is not a good friend. (non-restrictive)

Rules	Examples
Use *who* for people. *Who* can be used in restrictive and non-restrictive clauses.	Students **who live with American families** learn English quickly.
	Ronald Reagan, **who died in 2004**, was the 40th president of the United States.
Use *that* for people or things. *That* can't be used in non-restrictive clauses (use *which* instead).	There was no return address on the package **that arrived this morning**.
	Students **that live with American families** learn English quickly.
Use *which* for things. *Which* can be used in restrictive and non-restrictive clauses.	The book **which I just read** is by James Patterson.
	The package from Joan, **which arrived this morning**, contained books and a DVD.

Practice 1

Write the correct relative pronoun to complete each sentence. For some items, more than one correct answer is possible.

Example:

1 *Pierre is the waiter* <u>who</u> *served our meal.*

2 The woman _____ is buying coffee is from China.

3 I want a pet _____ doesn't make a lot of noise.

4 We changed planes in Reykjavik, _____ is the capital of Iceland.

5 I have a very strange neighbor _____ lives by herself and never talks to anybody.

6 Our teacher, _____ is very funny, uses jokes and stories to help us learn.

7 If you are sick, you should eat fruits _____ are rich in vitamins.

8 The Colorado River, _____ flows through seven U.S. states, is 2,334 km long.

9 The students made an appointment with Dr. Sedge, _____ is the president of the university.

10 The cat _____ is sleeping on my porch does not belong to me.

11 My neighbor has a 1965 Ford Mustang, _____ is a classic American car.

Practice 2

Circle the letter next to the correct form of the relative pronoun to complete the sentence.

Example:

1 *Mrs. Golden is the woman* _____ *sold me her old car.*
   (a) *who*
   b *which*

2 People _____ have diabetes should not eat sugar.
   a who
   b which

3 Public schools _____ require uniforms are becoming more common.
   a which
   b that

4 Mt. McKinley, _____ is in Alaska, is the highest mountain in the United States.

   a which

   b that

5 The child identified the dog _____ bit her.

   a which

   b that

6 The raccoon, _____ was as big as a dog, frightened me.

   a which

   b that

7 There is a special service for tourists _____ lose their passports.

   a who

   b which

8 We visited Yellowstone, _____ is the oldest national park in the United States.

   a which

   b that

9 The sperm whale, _____ is a mammal, has the largest brain of any animal.

   a which

   b that

10 The pyramids _____ are in Egypt are bigger than those in Central America.

   a which

   b that

11 Young people _____ join the army learn many useful skills.

   a who

   b which

The Complete Sentence
SUBJECT AND VERB

Subject and Verb

A **sentence** is a group of words that:

- has a subject and a verb
- expresses a complete idea
- begins with a capital letter and ends with a period, question mark, or exclamation point.

Rules	Examples
The subject tells who or what does something. It can be a noun or pronoun.	**The mail** arrived.
	They will not be at the meeting.
The subject can be a phrase.	**A beautiful horse** stood in the shade.
The subject may be compound (two or more nouns connected with *and* or *or*).	**Robert and Susan** were married last week.
There are two kinds of verbs. Action verbs express an action. Some action verbs are *walk*, *laugh*, *drive*, and *swim*.	George **carried** the baby.
Linking (or stative) verbs connect the subject and the rest of the sentence. They do not express an action. Some linking verbs are *be*, *seem*, *look*, *become*, *taste*, and *smell*.	The baby **seems** sick.
Verbs can be compound (more than one verb connected with *and*, *or*, or *but*).	Karen **paid** her bill **and left** the restaurant.

Practice 1

Circle the letter of the correct subject of each sentence.

Example:

1 *My aunt and uncle like coffee and tea.*
  a *my aunt*
  b *my uncle*
  (c) *my aunt and uncle*

2 The living room and the dining room are painted blue.
  a the living room
  b the dining room
  c the living room and the dining room

3 We planted roses and lilies in the front garden.
  a We
  b roses and lilies
  c the front garden

4 Every morning, Jack jumps out of bed and does 50 push-ups.
  a Every morning
  b Jack
  c bed

5 Our backyard has a picnic table, chairs, and a swing.
  a Our backyard
  b a picnic table
  c a swing

6 The traffic was terrible on Olympic Boulevard this morning.
  a The traffic
  b Olympic Boulevard
  c this morning

7 My daughter's school does not have a library.
  a My daughter
  b My daughter's school
  c a library

8 Those flowers attract bees and butterflies.
  a Those flowers
  b bees
  c butterflies

9 Visitors to the park must remember that bears are wild animals.

   a Visitors

   b the park

   c bears

10 Every house in town was damaged by the tornado.

   a Every house

   b town

   c the tornado

11 Joan and Alice will prepare the PowerPoint presentation for the meeting.

   a Joan and Alice

   b the PowerPoint presentation

   c meeting

Practice 2

Circle the letter next to the correct verb in each sentence. Some verbs are compound.

Example:

1 *My aunt and uncle like coffee and tea.*

   a *aunt*

   ⓑ *like*

   c *coffee*

2 Every morning, Jack jumps out of bed and does 50 push-ups.

   a jumps

   b does

   c jumps and does

3 On Saturdays, we sleep late and eat breakfast together.

   a sleep

   b eat

   c sleep and eat

4 Jack's car doesn't have a working air conditioner.

   a have

   b doesn't have

   c working

5 Wolfgang Amadeus Mozart wrote more than 600 musical compositions.

   a wrote

   b musical

   c compositions

6 I watched the waves.

   a watched

   b the

   c waves

7 My father always has a cup of coffee and a cookie after work.

   a always

   b has

   c work

8 We had a big family dinner and celebrated my sister's birthday.

   a had

   b celebrated

   c had and celebrated

9 My daughter's school does not have a library.

   a school

   b have

   c does not have

10 Sandra lives and works in a studio apartment.

   a lives

   b works

   c lives and works

11 Leo speaks and writes English perfectly.

   a speaks

   b writes

   c speaks and writes

SUBJECT-VERB AGREEMENT

Subject-Verb Agreement

In a sentence, the subject and verb must agree. This means you use a singular verb with a singular subject and a plural verb with a plural subject.

Rules	Examples
Use a singular verb with a singular count noun as a subject.	**Anna lives** on a farm.
	Pietro doesn't have a car.
	My house is very small.
Use a singular verb with a noncount noun as a subject.	**My apple juice is** too sweet.
	This coffee comes from Jamaica.
	Milk tastes good.
Use a plural verb with a plural count noun as a subject.	**Horses eat** grass.
	Horses don't eat meat.
	Apples are good for you.
Use a plural verb with a compound subject (a subject with two or more nouns joined with *and* or *or*).	**Tomatoes and avocados are** expensive now.
	The president and his wife always **eat** breakfast together.

Practice 1

Circle the letter next to the verb that agrees with the subject.

Example:

1 *Susan and George* _____ *three children.*
   (a) *have*
   b *has*

2 Senses _____ us enjoy food.
   a helps
   b help

3 Human beings _____ born with about 9000 taste buds.

   a are

   b is

4 This number _____ as we get older.

   a decreases

   b decrease

5 We _____ taste buds over time.

   a loses

   b lose

6 That's why many older people _____ that their food _____ no taste.

   a complain

   b complains

   c has

   d have

7 Traditional offices _____ enormous amounts of paper.

   a use

   b uses

8 They _____ a lot of space to store paper.

   a need

   b needs

9 Nowadays, more and more businesses _____ becoming paperless.

   a is

   b are

10 Many paperless offices _____ just a desk, a chair, and a computer.

   a have

   b has

11 All information _____ stored in digital form.

   a is

   b are

Practice 2

Write the correct form of the verb in parentheses to complete each sentence. Use the present tense.

Example:

1 Apples and oranges *have* (have) a lot of vitamin C.

2 Caffeine _____ (be) a stimulant.

3 Both coffee and tea _____ (contain) caffeine.

4 People _____ (drink) caffeine in coffee, tea, and many soft drinks.

5 A typical cup of coffee _____ (have) about 112 milligrams of caffeine.

6 Energy drinks _____ (have) about 80 milligrams of caffeine.

7 Americans _____ (drink) about 45 million pounds of caffeine each year.

8 Caffeine _____ (have) some health benefits.

9 For example, it _____ (help) people stay awake.

10 It also _____ (reduce) your chance of getting diabetes.

11 However, some people _____ (get) headaches if they stop drinking coffee.

SUBJECT, VERB, OBJECT

Presentation

Subject, Verb, Object

Every English sentence has a subject and a verb. A sentence can also have an **object**. An object receives the action of the verb. It can be a noun or pronoun.

The catcher (subject) dropped (verb) the baseball (object).

I (subject) love (verb) you (object).

Here are additional rules about objects.

Rules	Examples
Some verbs have objects. These verbs are called transitive verbs. Some examples of transitive verbs are *have, love, need, like, spend, put, buy, make, send, take,* and *want*.	Please **put the plates** on the table.
	I don't **want any coffee**.
	Do you **have any free time**?
Some verbs do not have objects. These verbs are called intransitive verbs. Some examples of intransitive verbs are *be, agree, come, fall, grow, happen, laugh, sit, sleep,* and *wait*.	The accident **happened** last night.
	The baby **is sleeping**.
Some verbs can be both transitive and intransitive. Some examples of these verbs are *answer, ask, finish, go, hit, learn, leave, move, order, sing, walk,* and *watch*.	The boy **answered *the question***. *(transitive)*
	I asked him a question, but he **didn't answer.** *(intransitive)*
English word order is almost always Subject–Verb–Object (SVO).	**I saw** a good **movie**.
Articles and adjectives can come before objects.	I'm going to buy **a new red sweater**.
Do not confuse the object of a verb with the object of a preposition in a prepositional phrase. A prepositional phrase begins with a preposition and ends with a noun or pronoun. The object of a verb receives the action of that verb.	I love **roller coasters**. *(object of the verb)*
	I agree with **you**. *(object of the preposition)*

Practice 1

Underline the object in each sentence.

1 Last month I spent too much money.

2 We ordered tickets for the concert.

3 John doesn't like his wife's political opinions.

4 Did your parrot learn any new words?

5 My cat walks around the house at night. He often makes a lot of noise.

6 Why did you put the keys in the refrigerator?

7 Green is a very relaxing color. Do you like it?

8 I need to finish the project before the end of the month.

9 The baseball hit the man on the head.

10 Gayle has 500 songs on her iPod.

11 The weather was terrible, so we watched movies on television all weekend.

Practice 2

Write the words in the correct subject-verb-object order.

1 _____

keys   my   I   lost

2 _____

piano   Indira   plays   the

3 _____

his   Mark   finish   didn't   homework

4 _____

new   we   a   need   car

5 _____

I   any   have   time   free   don't

6 _____

loves   Zara   bread   and   butter

7 _____

can   bring   me   water   of   glass   you   a

8 _____

the   all   students   passed

9 _____

more   has   10,000   lakes   Minnesota   than

10 _____

an   hour   Tom   left   ago

11 _____

about   Frost   Robert   America   many   poems   wrote

FRAGMENTS

Presentation

Fragments

A *fragment* is an incomplete part of something. In writing, a fragment is an incomplete sentence that is missing either the subject, the verb, or the independent clause.

Fragments	Examples / Solutions
Missing subject	<u>Correct:</u> **It** is fun to swim in the lake.
	<u>Incorrect:</u> Is fun to swim in the lake.
Missing verb	<u>Correct:</u> Yellowstone **is** America's oldest national park.
	<u>Incorrect:</u> Yellowstone America's oldest national park.
Adjective clause with missing independent clause	<u>Correct:</u> My brother, who is six and a half feet tall, **is always uncomfortable on airplanes**.
	<u>Incorrect:</u> My brother, who is six and a half feet tall.
Phrase without an independent clause	<u>Correct:</u> **Americans enjoy driving foreign cars**, for example, Toyotas, Volkswagens, and Audis.
	<u>Incorrect:</u> For example, Toyotas, Volkswagens, and Audis.

Practice 1

Circle the letter next to the error in each fragment.

Example:

1 *The last subway train at 11 p.m.*
   a *Missing subject*
   (b) *Missing verb*
   c *Adjective clause with missing independent clause*
   d *Phrase without an independent clause*

2 who gave me the money.
   a Missing subject
   b Missing verb
   c Adjective clause with missing independent clause
   d Phrase without an independent clause

3 Is possible to buy almost anything at an American drugstore.
   a Missing subject
   b Missing verb
   c Adjective clause with missing independent clause
   d Phrase without an independent clause

4 For example dogs.
   a Missing subject
   b Missing verb
   c Adjective clause with missing independent clause
   d Phrase without an independent clause

5 Mr. Tyler, he a good English teacher.
   a Missing subject
   b Missing verb
   c Adjective clause with missing independent clause
   d Phrase without an independent clause

6 which I was trying to tell you.
   a Missing subject
   b Missing verb
   c Adjective clause with missing independent clause
   d Phrase without an independent clause

7 Istanbul a fascinating city to visit.
   a Missing subject
   b Missing verb
   c Adjective clause with missing independent clause
   d Phrase without an independent clause

8 Don't need a car in New York City.

  a Missing subject

  b Missing verb

  c Adjective clause with missing independent clause

  d Phrase without an independent clause

9 Who live in tropical countries.

  a Missing subject

  b Missing verb

  c Adjective clause with missing independent clause

  d Phrase without an independent clause

10 They not.

  a Missing subject

  b Missing verb

  c Adjective clause with missing independent clause

  d Phrase without an independent clause

11 In the state of Wyoming.

  a Missing subject

  b Missing verb

  c Adjective clause with missing independent clause

  d Phrase without an independent clause

Practice 2

Underline the fragments in each paragraph.

1 Los Angeles is an international city with immigrants from all over the world. Many of these immigrants live in special neighborhoods. For example, Chinatown. Has Chinese restaurants, clothing stores, bakeries, banks, gift shops, and more. Many people in Chinatown don't speak English. Because they don't need it. Is possible to get almost any kind of Chinese product or service in Chinatown. Without traveling to China.

2 Is fun to visit Los Angeles. If you have a car. If not, you will need to use public transportation. Which is not fast or convenient. Los Angeles has a new subway system, but it does not travel to many important places. Such as the airport. There is no elevated train or streetcars. There are buses, but they are slow. Because traffic is heavy. Especially in the early morning and late afternoon. When people are traveling to and from work.

RUN-ON SENTENCES

Presentation

Run-On Sentences

A *run-on sentence* is a sentence error. It happens when you join two or more simple sentences without any conjunctions or punctuation.

There are two ways to correct or prevent a run-on sentence:

Rules	Examples
End the first independent clause with a period and start the other with a capital letter.	<u>Correct</u>: My sister is a nurse**.** **S**he works 60 hours a week.
	<u>Incorrect</u>: My sister is a nurse she works 60 hours a week.
Insert a comma and a coordinating conjunction between independent clauses. A comma is not enough.	<u>Correct</u>: My sister is a nurse, **and** she works 60 hours a week.
	<u>Incorrect</u>: My sister is a nurse she works 60 hours a week.
	<u>Incorrect</u>: My sister is a nurse, she works 60 hours a week.

Practice 1

Read the sentence. Circle the letter that identifies each sentence as correct or incorrect.

Example:

1 *My uncle is a diplomat he travels all over the world.*

   a *Correct*

   ⓑ *Incorrect*

2 I'm not home now please leave a message.

   a Correct

   b Incorrect

3 I stayed in the sun too long, so I got a sunburn.

   a Correct

   b Incorrect

4 Some people like to read others prefer to watch television.
- **a** Correct
- **b** Incorrect

5 Please close the door it's windy.
- **a** Correct
- **b** Incorrect

6 Broccoli is a very healthy vegetable. It is rich in calcium and vitamins.
- **a** Correct
- **b** Incorrect

7 I have black hair my sister is a blonde.
- **a** Correct
- **b** Incorrect

8 Don't sit like that it's bad for your back.
- **a** Correct
- **b** Incorrect

9 I like strawberries, but I am allergic to them.
- **a** Correct
- **b** Incorrect

10 This is my sister Hannah she's a doctor.
- **a** Correct
- **b** Incorrect

11 Bicycles are convenient, but they aren't safe in the city.
- **a** Correct
- **b** Incorrect

Practice 2

Underline the correct sentence in each set of three.

1 It's going to rain. Close the windows.
It's going to rain, close the windows.
It's going to rain close the windows.

2 Hue-Ya plays the violin, and she also sings.
Hue-Ya plays the violin, she also sings.
Hue-Ya plays the violin she also sings.

3 Sami fell asleep in class, everyone laughed.
Sami fell asleep in class everyone laughed.
Sami fell asleep in class, and everyone laughed.

4 Let's go home I'm tired.

Let's go home. I'm tired.

Let's go home, I'm tired.

5 The lake is wide it's not very deep.

The lake is wide, it's not very deep.

The lake is wide, but it's not very deep.

6 A dog was barking all night I couldn't sleep.

A dog was barking all night, I couldn't sleep.

A dog was barking all night, so I couldn't sleep.

7 The basketball player was huge. He was more than 7 feet tall.

The basketball player was huge he was more than 7 feet tall.

The basketball player was huge, he was more than 7 feet tall.

8 Garlic tastes wonderful it's also very healthy.

Garlic tastes wonderful, it's also very healthy.

Garlic tastes wonderful. It's also very healthy.

9 Ms. Saroyan got a job in Ankara. It is the capital of Turkey.

Ms. Saroyan got a job in Ankara, it is the capital of Turkey.

Ms. Saroyan got a job in Ankara it is the capital of Turkey.

10 I'm so glad that movie is over let's go.

I'm so glad that movie is over. Let's go.

I'm so glad that movie is over, let's go.

11 We followed the GPS, but we got lost anyway.

We followed the GPS, we got lost anyway.

We followed the GPS we got lost anyway.

COMMA SPLICES

Presentation

Comma Splices

To join two independent clauses, you cannot use a comma alone. This results in a **comma splice**. There are three ways to correct or prevent a comma splice:

Rules	Examples
Replace the comma with a period.	<u>Correct</u>: I found a dog**.** I brought him home with me.
	<u>Incorrect</u>: I found a dog**,** I brought him home with me.
Add a conjunction (*and, or, but, so*) after the comma.	<u>Correct</u>: We needed lettuce, **so** I went to the store.
	<u>Incorrect</u>: We needed lettuce, I went to the store.
Change one of the clauses into a dependent clause.	<u>Correct</u>: **Since we shopped all day**, we were very tired.
	<u>Incorrect</u>: We shopped all day, we were very tired.

Practice 1

Read each item. Circle the letter next to the correct answer.

Example:

1 *My shoes were wet, I took them off.*
  (a) *comma splice*
  b *correct sentence*

2 Ballroom dancing is fun, it's good exercise.
  a comma splice
  b correct sentence

3 Karina likes to dance, but her husband doesn't.
  a comma splice
  b correct sentence

4 Don't leave your shoes in the hallway, put them away.
  a comma splice
  b correct sentence

5 Since he's afraid of elevators, David always takes the stairs.
  a comma splice
  b correct sentence

6 The U.S. flag is red, white, and blue. The Italian flag is red, white, and green.
  a comma splice
  b correct sentence

7 Ricky is never cold, he wears shorts all year round.
  a comma splice
  b correct sentence

8 Americans usually shake hands when they meet for the first time.
  a comma splice
  b correct sentence

9 I answered the phone, no one was there.
  a comma splice
  b correct sentence

10 Marta is Polish, her husband is French.
  a comma splice
  b correct sentence

11 My dog can swim, but he hates the water.
  a comma splice
  b correct sentence

Practice 2

In each set, two choices are correct. Underline the sentence that is incorrect.

1 Joe is American, but he works in Canada.
Joe is American, he works in Canada.
Joe is American. He works in Canada.

2 We went to our first baseball game. It was very slow.
We went to our first baseball game, it was very slow.
We went to our first baseball game, and it was very slow.

3 I have a toothache. I need to see a dentist.
I have a toothache, so I need to see a dentist.
I have a toothache, I need to see a dentist.

4 Since baby rabbits are blind, they depend on their mothers for everything.

Baby rabbits are blind, they depend on their mothers for everything.

Baby rabbits are blind. They depend on their mothers for everything.

5 Steven finished his algebra class. Then he took geometry.

Steven finished his algebra class, then he took geometry.

After Steven finished his algebra class, he took geometry.

6 As soon as we walked into the house, we turned on the air conditioner.

We walked into the house, we turned on the air conditioner.

We walked into the house, and we turned on the air conditioner.

7 I stopped taking violin lessons, I never practiced.

I stopped taking violin lessons because I never practiced.

I stopped taking violin lessons. I never practiced.

8 There are over a hundred billionaires in the world, only a few are women.

There are over a hundred billionaires in the world. Only a few are women.

There are over a hundred billionaires in the world, but only a few are women.

9 The war ended, and all the soldiers went home.

As soon as the war ended, all the soldiers went home.

The war ended, all the soldiers went home.

10 Alice turned 16, she got a job at a candy store.

When Alice turned 16, she got a job at a candy store.

Alice turned 16. Then she got a job at a candy store.

11 Millions of people enjoy shopping online, it's easy and fast.

Millions of people enjoy shopping online because it's easy and fast.

Millions of people enjoy shopping online. It's easy and fast.

PARAGRAPH ORGANIZATION

Topic Sentence

Practice 1

Read the topic sentence. Underline the controlling idea.

1 I admire my grandparents because they are generous and hardworking.

2 Loss of habitat and hunting caused the extinction of the Javan tiger in the early 1980s.

3 Vitamin D is necessary for good health.

4 Hawaii is the perfect place to go for your honeymoon.

5 The Department of Water and Power offers these tips to help you lower your water bill.

6 Talent, dedication, and luck are three characteristics of professional musicians.

7 Swimming has health benefits for people of all ages.

8 Hawaii is the perfect place to go for a winter vacation.

9 Growing rare flowers is very hard to do and takes a lot of work.

10 For the best selection and lowest prices, shop at Hart's Grocery Store.

11 Computer viruses cause people to lose both time and money.

Practice 2

Read each paragraph. Circle the letter next to the best topic sentence.

1 _____ First, they must be excellent writers. They have to be able to write quickly and without errors in order to meet their deadlines. Second, journalists must have good interviewing skills. They need to be comfortable speaking to strangers, and, at the same time, know how to get people to talk to them. Also, journalists need to have knowledge about many topics, including geography, history, business, and science. For this reason, nearly all journalists these days are college graduates. Finally, today's journalists must be comfortable with technology. They need to know how to operate cameras and recording devices; in addition, they need to have excellent computer skills.

a Journalists today need to have a number of essential skills.

b I plan to go to college and major in journalism.

c I admire journalists for several reasons.

2 _____ For example, Barrow, the northernmost city in Alaska, has a polar climate. The average winter temperature is −16 degrees F, and the average summer temperature is 8 degrees. Barrow has about 5 inches of rain a year. Spring is the most popular season. In contrast, Ketchikan, located in the south of Alaska, has a temperate climate. The average winter temperature is 35 degrees, and the average temperature in summer is a "warm" 58 degrees. Summer is the most popular season in southern Alaska—but watch out for the mosquitoes!

a I am planning a driving trip from Barrow to Ketchikan, Alaska.

b Because of the freezing climate, some parts of Alaska have almost no people.

c Alaska is a huge state with several different types of climate.

3 _____ She was born on July 24, 1898, in the state of Kansas. Amelia was interested in flying from the time she was a small child. However, in those days it was almost impossible for a woman to be a pilot. Amelia worked as a social worker and as a nurse, and she learned how to fly as a hobby. In 1932, she became the first woman to fly across the Atlantic Ocean alone. A year later, she flew solo from Hawaii to the U.S. mainland. In June 1937, she took off from Miami, Florida, in an attempt to become the first person to fly around the world near the equator. Tragically, her plane disappeared on July 1. It was never found.

a I'm reading a book about Amelia Earhart.

b Amelia Earhart lived a short but inspiring life.

c Amelia Earhart came from a small town.

4 _____ First of all, my energy level has increased. I used to take a nap every afternoon, but now I can study, work, and play sports, and I never feel tired during the daytime. Since I don't take naps anymore, I have more time to do the things I want to do. My ability to concentrate has also improved. I can read faster and do my homework in less time than before. As a result, my schoolwork has improved. Best of all, I feel calmer and happier than before. All my friends have noticed this change in me. My advice to anyone who wants to feel better is this: Stop eating sugar! It might change your life!

a My physical, mental, and emotional health have improved since I stopped eating sugar.

b Three years ago I changed the way I eat.

c There are three reasons why sugar is bad for you.

5 _____ To begin, our taxi broke down on the way to the airport. As a result, we missed our plane to Miami and had to wait several hours for another flight. When we finally arrived at our hotel in Miami, we were told that our reservations were cancelled because we were late. We finally got another room after arguing with the manager for 20 minutes. The second day we were in Miami, someone broke into our hotel room while we were at the beach and stole our clothes and some jewelry. Then it rained nonstop for the next three days, so we couldn't go to the beach at all. When we finally returned home, we discovered that a water pipe had broken, and all the rooms downstairs were flooded. In sum, this was the worst vacation of our entire lives.

a Last month we went to Florida on vacation.

b Miami is a popular place to take a family vacation.

c Our family vacation in Florida last month was a disaster.

Ordering

TIME ORDER

Presentation

Ordering by Time

Paragraphs usually contain one idea introduced by a topic sentence. The topic sentence introduces the paragraph and is followed by supporting sentences. The paragraph ends with a concluding sentence. Two kinds of paragraphs are organized by time: narrative and process.

- A **narrative** paragraph tells a story or describes a sequence of events.
- A **process** paragraph explains the steps you must follow to do or make something.
- Both types of paragraphs begin with the first event and describe each of the following events in order.

Both narrative and process paragraphs use time-order signals to help readers follow the order of events or steps. There are many different types of time-order signals. For example:

Notice:

- Use a comma after most signal words (Exceptions: *then* and *soon*).

Example: It's easy to grow tomatoes. *First of all*, fill a large pot with dirt. …

- Prepositional phrases can come in different places in a sentence.

Example: On June 4, a terrible hurricane struck Charleston. / A terrible hurricane struck Charleston on June 4.

Signal Words	Prepositional Phrases
first, first of all	in the morning, afternoon, night
to begin	at 8:00 a.m.
second, third, etc.	on March 4
soon	in 1987
now	at the time
next, (one hour) later, then	after (a while), after that
finally	before lunch

Practice 1

Circle ten signal words or prepositional phrases of time in the following paragraph.

This is how Melinda studies for a test. To begin, she sits at her desk and organizes her papers and books. She does this because she can't concentrate if her desk is messy. Soon she decides that she needs a cup of coffee. Therefore, she goes to the kitchen, boils water, and prepares her drink. Next, she decides that she's hungry, so she makes a sandwich, too. After that, she returns to her room and turns on her computer. Five minutes later, her phone rings. It's her friend Mary Ellen, who wants to talk about their plans for the weekend. They chat for a few minutes, and then Melinda ends the conversation and starts studying. But after a while, she starts to feel sleepy, so she decides to take a nap. She lies down and quickly falls asleep. Two hours later, Melinda wakes up in a panic. She quickly washes her face, drinks some water and finally, she returns to her desk. After 20 minutes, Melinda looks at the clock and sees that it's time for her favorite television program. So, she sighs, closes her books, and decides to postpone her studying until tomorrow.

Practice 2

Part 1

Read the topic sentence. Then choose how the four sentences should be ordered after the topic sentence.

Topic sentence: Pesto is a delicious sauce that you can eat with pasta. It's very easy to make.

1 Finally, pour the mixture into a bowl and put it in the refrigerator for a couple of hours.
- **a** first
- **b** second
- **c** third
- **d** fourth

2 Second, chop the garlic and pine nuts with a sharp knife. Put the chopped ingredients with half of the olive oil in a food processor and blend everything well.
- **a** first
- **b** second
- **c** third
- **d** fourth

3 Before you start, make sure you have the following ingredients: 2 cups of basil leaves, 2 cloves of garlic, 1/2 cup parmesan cheese, 2/3 cup olive oil, 1/4 cup pine nuts, salt and pepper.
- **a** first
- **b** second
- **c** third
- **d** fourth

4 To begin, put the pine nuts on a baking sheet and toast them for 5 or 10 minutes. Their color will be golden brown.

   a first

   b second

   c third

   d fourth

Part 2

Read the topic sentence. Then choose how the four sentences should be ordered after the topic sentence.

Topic sentence: I spent yesterday morning having fun with my sister.

1 My sister had an appointment after lunch, so we said good-bye and made plans to get together again soon.

   a first

   b second

   c third

   d fourth

2 To start the day, she came to my house and I made waffles with whipped cream and strawberries. They were delicious!

   a first

   b second

   c third

   d fourth

3 After we ate, we took my dog for a walk around the neighborhood. We saw some neighbors, and I introduced my sister to them.

   a first

   b second

   c third

   d fourth

4 Next, we decided to go for a swim at the public swimming pool.

   a first

   b second

   c third

   d fourth

LISTING BY ORDER OF IMPORTANCE

Listing by Order of Importance

In a listing-order paragraph, you divide the topic into segments. These segments may describe, for example, types, groups, characteristics, reasons, ways of doing something, examples, advantages, or disadvantages.

Some paragraphs list the points in order of importance. Some discuss the least important point first and the most important point last. Some discuss the most important point first and the least important point last.

Use signal words and phrases like these to list items by order of importance:

Signal Words and Phrases for Order of Importance		
first, second, third, etc.	one (way, reason, etc.)	the most important (reason, point, advantage, etc.)
first of all, to begin	another (example, characteristic, etc.)	most importantly
next, also, in addition, finally	the next (point, problem, etc.)	most of all

Practice 1

Write the signal words and phrases that correctly complete each sentence in the paragraph.

Another way	One reason	Most importantly	To begin
First of all	Finally	Third	Also
Most of all	For one thing	In addition	
Next	In conclusion	Second	

Paragraph 1

If you would like to become a better cook, there are four things you can try. _____ , if you have time, watch cooking shows on television. Such shows are both entertaining and educational. _____ to watch is to learn how to chop vegetables quickly and easily. _____, use recipe books. Such books are especially useful for beginning cooks, but experienced cooks use them, too. _____ , try cooking with a friend. My friend Ben, for example, is a terrific cook. I have prepared many meals with him. By watching him, I learned several tasty ways to cook fish. _____ , don't be afraid to experiment. Try out new spices or different combinations of spices. Mix foods in a new way. Some of your experiments may be unsuccessful, but some of them may result in tasty dishes that all your friends will want to make!

Paragraph 2

Several characteristics give camels the ability to survive in the hot deserts of the Middle East. _____ , camels have long, thin legs, and their feet end in wide pads that help them move easily over sand. Therefore, desert people such as Bedouins use camels for transportation to this day. _____ , camels can eat dry, sharp bushes that sheep and goats refuse to eat. They can do this because their lips are covered in stiff, hard hairs. These hairs allow the animals to push their noses through the bushes and break off the plants. _____ , their mouths have a special shape to allow them to chew these bushes. _____ , camels have the ability to go for a long time without water – as long as fifty days in winter and five days in summer. These characteristics explain why camels are perfectly designed for life in the desert.

Practice 2

Write the number for each sentence in the correct order to form a paragraph organized by order of importance. Some of them have been done for you.

_____ First, she is very knowledgeable.

_____ She knows how to teach classes for many different ages and ability levels.

_____ There are two characteristics that make my zumba teacher, Marcella, one of the best dance teachers I've ever had.

__7__ This makes everybody want to try harder.

_____ Second, Marcella is enthusiastic.

_____ While we are dancing, she constantly shouts out encouraging words to anyone who is tired or slow.

__4__ For example, one of the classes she teaches is called Zumba Gold, which is mainly for older people.

SPATIAL ORDERING

Spatial Ordering

Spatial ordering means organizing details according to their location.

The topic sentence for a spatial paragraph should:

- mention the space you are describing
- make a comment about it

You can organize details in the following ways. You can also use a combination of these ways. For example, if you are looking at an open refrigerator, you could describe the items on each shelf from top to bottom and from left to right (or right to left).

Organizing by Spatial Ordering			
top to bottom	far to near	right to left	outside to inside
bottom to top	near to far	left to right	inside to outside
north to south	east to west	clockwise	
south to north	west to east	counter-clockwise	

Practice 1

Read the paragraph. Circle the letter that identifies the type of space ordering used in each one. An item can have more than one correct answer.

1 I have an old jewelry box that I got from my grandmother. It is divided into two parts, and each part opens with a door. If you open the door on the right, you see an open space. Near the top there is a kind of carousel with hooks for hanging necklaces. You can turn the carousel to reach the necklace you want to wear. If you open the door on the left, you see a stack of five small drawers. I keep rings in the top drawer. The second drawer contains bracelets. The third contains hair pins and clips. The fourth contains a broken necklace, and the fifth is empty. I keep this jewelry box on top of my dresser, and I use it every day.

    a right to left

    b outside to inside

    c top to bottom

2 My veterinarian's office is organized very efficiently. Coming through the front door, you enter a waiting area with plastic sofas. Several clients are usually waiting there with their dogs or cats. Opposite the entrance, on the far side of the waiting room, there is a counter where the receptionist sits and does her work. Behind the counter there is a door, and behind the door there is a hall with rooms on both sides. First there are examination rooms. These are where the veterinarian examines animals and does simple procedures. Farther down the hall, there is a surgery suite consisting of an operating room and a recovery room. Finally, at the end of the hall, there is a restroom and the veterinarian's office.

  a left to right

  b far to near

  c front to back

3 The dining room is my favorite room in my house. The room is about 12 square feet. In the center there is a beautiful, oval, wood dining table surrounded by eight comfortable wood chairs. There are large windows on the east and south walls. These windows allow light to enter the room almost all day. Between the two windows on the east wall there are two wonderful paintings that I bought while I was traveling in Macedonia. They show peaceful mountain views. On the west side of the dining room there is a large cabinet for storing dishes. There is also a door leading to the kitchen. Finally, the north wall has an arch connecting the dining room to the living room, as well as two bookcases full of books about art, travel, and history. The dining room is painted a soft, sand color. It is a pleasure to spend time there, even if I am not eating.

  a right to left

  b inside to outside

  c clockwise

Practice 2

Circle the letter that identifies the best topic sentence for the spatial paragraphs.

1 _____ The one farthest to the north borders Canada and is called Washington. It has 71,300 square miles and a population of almost 7 million people. Washington state receives an average of 38.15 inches of rain a year. South of Washington is the state of Oregon, with an area of about 98,000 square miles but only about 4 million people. Oregon has an average annual rainfall of 27 inches. South of Oregon is California, the third-largest state in the United States. It has an area of 163,696 square miles and about 38 million people. California gets an average of only about 22 inches of rain each year.

  a A driving trip from California to Washington can be a fantastic vacation.

  b Only three states border the Pacific Ocean on the west coast of the United States.

  c California has the best weather of any U.S. state.

2 _____ It is a long, narrow space located between the kitchen and the back door. One wall has storage cabinets on top. Under the cabinets there are hooks for hanging shopping bags, wet coats, and the dog's leash. Under these hooks there is a bench where we can sit and change our shoes. There is storage space for shoes and boots under the bench. Opposite this wall my parents have their washing machine and dryer. Above these machines there are racks for hanging wet clothes, and next to the washing machine there is a deep sink where we can wash our dog. As you can imagine, the service porch is a very important room in my parents' house.

  a The service porch in my parent's house has several functions.

  b There is a room in my parents' house that we almost never use.

  c You must use the back door if you enter my parents' house with wet shoes.

Cause and Effect

INTRODUCING CAUSES

Presentation

Introducing Causes

A **cause paragraph** talks about the reasons why something (called an *effect*) happens.

- The topic sentence mentions a problem or situation. The controlling idea states that there are one or more causes. For example:

  There are several causes of asthma in children.
  I discontinued my membership at Fitness Gym for three reasons.
  Linda moved back to her hometown for many reasons.

- The supporting sentences in the paragraph discuss the causes. There should be one or more sentences for each cause. Use listing signals (*first, the first cause, second, next, the last cause*) to introduce each one.

- The conclusion should repeat or summarize the main idea and offer a final comment or suggestion.

Use the following signal words and phrases to introduce causes:

Signal Words and Phrases	Examples
because, since	We stayed home **because / since** it was raining.
because of, due to, as a result of	We couldn't go out **because of / due to / as a result of** the snow.

Practice 1

Read the outlines. For each outline, underline all the causes that support the topic sentence.

Paragraph 1

Topic sentence: I planned to marry my boyfriend, Charles, but there are three reasons why we decided to break up and not get married.

We have different opinions about politics.

I want to have a big family, but Charles doesn't like children.

Although we broke up, we are still good friends. We always got along well.

Charles wants to live in a big city, but I prefer to live in a small town.

Paragraph 2

Topic sentence: I am never going to eat at the Rodeo Café again for three reasons.

The Rodeo Café is only three blocks from my house, so I don't need to drive there.

The café has free WiFi.

The café is dirty. The chairs and tables are sticky, and the bathrooms are disgusting.

The café plays great country music.

The café raised its prices recently. For example, a hamburger now costs $9, and a small salad is $4.50. That's too much.

The waiters aren't serious about their work. They talk on their cell phones instead of serving customers.

Paragraph 3

Topic sentence: Rappos.com is the number one online shoe store in the country for several reasons.

Their prices are a little higher than other online shoe sellers.

It is easy to order and return shoes.

They have a huge selection of shoes for men, women, and children.

If they don't have the shoes you want in your size, they will get them for you.

If you need help, you can always reach a friendly, helpful salesperson.

People don't like to shop online.

Practice 2

Read the paragraphs. In each paragraph, underline one sentence that does not belong.

Paragraph 1

There are three main causes of forest fires in the western part of the United States. First, many forest fires start because of natural reasons, such as lightning. When lightning strikes a tree, it can catch on fire. Then because the weather in the West is often very dry and windy, the fire can spread very quickly to other trees. Another cause of forest fires is careless human activity, such as smoking. If somebody throws a cigarette on the ground in a hot, dry forest, nearby bushes and leaves can easily catch fire. The fire can then spread to the trees. People should not smoke at all because smoking has so many bad effects on people and the environment. A third cause of forest fires is arson. Arson is when a person starts a fire on purpose. Arson fires cause millions of dollars in damage to forests and homes every year. Whatever the cause, forest fires are a real danger in the American West. It is important to know what causes them, so we can prevent them as much as possible.

Paragraph 2

Many adults suffer from back pain for several reasons. First, some people get back pain because of the type of job they have. If they have a job that involves lifting, pulling, or pushing things, these activities can twist the spine and can cause back pain. Also, people who sit at a desk all day may get back pain if their chairs are not comfortable, or if they stay still for too long. In addition, many people who sit and work at a computer all day may develop problems with their eyes and their weight. Another reason for back pain is the way that people carry things. If people carry a heavy bag on one shoulder every day, or a heavy child, it puts a lot of stress on the muscles and the spine. This might cause back pain. Finally, people can also get back pain because of bad posture, which means they don't sit or stand straight. In summary, back pain is a real problem for many adults. Understanding the causes of back pain can help them to change bad habits and live healthier, pain-free lives.

INTRODUCING EFFECTS

Presentation

Introducing Effects

An **effect** is the result of a cause. A paragraph can include one or more causes and effects of those causes.

- The topic sentence states the cause. The controlling idea states that there are one or more effects. For example:

Singing can have a number of positive effects on people's health.

The slow economy has hurt my hometown in three ways.

Forest fires in the southwest part of the state have had terrible effects on wildlife, plant life, and tourism.

- The supporting sentences discuss the effects. There should be one or more sentences for each one. Use listing signals (*first, the first effect, second, next, the last effect*) to introduce each one.

- The conclusion should summarize the main idea and offer a final comment, suggestion, etc.

Use the following signal words and phrases to introduce effects:

Signal Words and Phrases	Examples
therefore, consequently, as a result	It was snowing hard. As a result, we canceled our shopping trip.
	Howard broke his leg. Consequently, he's using crutches to get around.
so	It snowed six inches last night, so most schools are closed today.

Practice 1

Read the outlines. Underline all the effects that properly support the topic sentence.

Paragraph 1

Topic sentence: Living in my own apartment has had three positive effects on my life.

I am paying for my own rent and bills, so I am learning how to manage money.

I am learning how to cook because my mother isn't here to prepare food for me.

Living alone can be boring.

I can be more independent. For example, I can decide for myself when I will go out, come home, and get up in the morning.

Many of my close friends are still living at home with their parents.

Paragraph 2

Topic sentence: Owning a pet can have many positive effects.

Pets help reduce stress.

Around 63 percent of American homes have at least one pet.

People who own pets are less lonely.

People with pets recover from illness faster.

It is illegal to keep "exotic" animals like lions as pets.

Children who live in a home with pets have fewer allergies.

Paragraph 3

Topic sentence: Participating in sports has many positive effects on children and teenagers.

Many young people play sports because they enjoy competition.

Sports help young people develop strength and flexibility.

I wasn't a good student in high school, but I was an excellent swimmer.

Playing a team sport teaches young people how to be fair and how to cooperate with others.

Young people who play sports are very busy. Therefore, they spend less time watching television and playing video games.

Practice 2

Read the paragraphs. In each paragraph, underline one sentence that does not belong.

Paragraph 1

The financial crisis of 2008 has had some serious negative effects on American people, businesses, and towns. One of the most serious effects is that millions of people have lost their jobs. As a result, many people have also lost their homes because they couldn't pay their mortgage. Also, many high school graduates have cancelled their college plans because they can't afford the cost of tuition. In addition, many college graduates are living with their parents again because they can't find jobs. My cousin, for example, is living with his parents, and he's using his time to develop several new software products. The weak economy has also had a negative effect on businesses. Many people are unemployed; therefore, they can't afford to buy new cars, eat in restaurants, or take vacations. For this reason, many businesses have failed since 2008. Finally, the weak economy has hurt many cities. When people are unemployed, they don't pay taxes. As a result, cities don't have money to pay teachers, fix roads, or provide services to poor people. In conclusion, the financial crisis of 2008 has had a devastating effect on the American economy.

Paragraph 2

For many women in developing countries, going to school and getting an education have positive effects on their lives and on their society. First, education influences the size and health of women's families. Women who go to school usually get married later and have fewer babies. Since they have smaller families, they can pay more attention to their children, and they have more money to pay for their care and schooling. In many African countries, many children only go to school for three years. Another positive effect of education for women is that they learn skills that can help them get jobs or start businesses. As a result, they are able to make money for their families. Finally, because educated women have smaller families and can make money for themselves, they have more money to spend. This can help them escape poverty and strengthen their local economy. In conclusion, it is clear that educating women has a lot of benefits for developing nations.

Comparison and Contrast
COMPARISON

Presentation

Comparison

In a paragraph of comparison, you talk about ways that two or more things are similar.

- The topic sentence names the things you are comparing and states how you plan to compare them. For example: *Seattle, Washington, and London, England, have similar weather.*

- All the sentences in the paragraph should talk about similarities. There should be no sentences about differences.

Here are some common expressions you can use to signal comparisons. Notice the grammar and punctuation of each word and phrase.

Signal Words and Phrases	Examples
similar to, like	The weather in Seattle, Washington, is **similar to / like** the weather in London, England.
also	Seattle has cool, rainy days all year long. London **also** has many cool, wet days.
alike, similar	Arabic and Hebrew are **similar / alike** in many ways.
both	**Both** Arabic and Hebrew have sounds pronounced in the back of the throat.
the same	Hebrew and Arabic came from **the same** ancient language.
similarly	Hebrew belongs to the Semitic language family. **Similarly**, Arabic is a Semitic language.

Practice 1

Read the outline for the comparison paragraph. In each outline, underline all the sentences that support the topic sentence.

1 **Topic sentence:** Mark and Jennifer are cousins, but many people think they are brother and sister because they look so much alike.

Mark is tall and athletic. Similarly, Jennifer is tall, and she's very good at sports.

Both Mark and Jennifer have curly blond hair and green eyes.

Mark wears glasses, but Jennifer doesn't.

Mark has freckles, and Jennifer does, too.

The way they walk is also very similar.

Concluding sentence: Because of all these similarities, it's hard for people to believe that Mark and Jennifer aren't siblings.

2 **Topic sentence:** Rebecca is a teller at City Bank, and George is a teller at National Bank. Their jobs are very similar.

Rebecca works more hours each week than George does.

Their salaries are almost the same. Each of them received a starting salary of about $10.00 per hour.

Their jobs offer similar benefits, too. Each of them receives health insurance, five days of sick leave, and two weeks of paid vacation per year.

Rebecca's boss is patient and supportive, but George's boss is often in a bad mood.

Concluding sentence: Both Rebecca and George plan to work for a year and then return to college in order to get more training in business.

3 **Topic sentence:** There are a number of similarities between cleaning my house and working in my garden.

On a hot day, I would rather clean my house than work outside in the garden.

Both activities are excellent forms of exercise.

House cleaning involves lots of bending and lifting. For example, I need to lift baskets of laundry and bend down to clean the floor.

Similarly, I need to bend down to pull weeds in the garden, and I have to carry sacks of fertilizer.

House cleaning is like gardening because both activities make my home more beautiful.

I get a chance to talk to my neighbors when I'm working in my garden.

Concluding sentence: Because I enjoy cleaning my house and gardening, I do these activities myself instead of paying someone else to do them.

Practice 2

Read the comparison paragraph. Circle the letter of the best topic sentence for the paragraph.

1 _____ First, the two sports have the same objective: to score a goal by putting a ball into a net. In each sport, a goal is equal to one point. The judges in both sports are called referees, and a referee can call a penalty or foul if a player breaks the rules of the game. Soccer is a very physical game, and it is easy for players to get injured. Similarly, water polo can be a very rough sport even though it is played in water. I have played both water polo and soccer since I was ten years old, and I love both games equally.

a Water polo and soccer appear to be very different sports, but they are similar in several ways.

b Two of my favorite sports are soccer and water polo.

c I play water polo and soccer at different times of the year.

2 _____ In fact, they are almost the same genetically. To begin, both dogs and wolves have 42 teeth, and both animal species are meat eaters. Like wolves, dogs have excellent senses of hearing and smell. Dogs and wolves are also similar in the way they communicate. When they hear something, their ears stand up. When they are afraid, their tail goes down. Finally, neither dogs nor wolves have sweat glands, so they must pant in order to release heat from their bodies. These similarities are not surprising because dogs descended from wolves only about 15,000 years ago.

a Many people have attempted to raise wolves as pets.

b Wolves and dogs are alike in many ways.

c My neighbor has a dog that is part wolf.

CONTRAST

Copyright © 2017 by Pearson Education, Inc. Duplication is not permitted.

Presentation

Contrast

In a paragraph of contrast, you talk about ways that two things are different.

- The topic sentence names the two things you are contrasting. The controlling idea states how they are different. For example: *Seattle, Washington, and Los Angeles, California, have very different weather.*

- The supporting sentences should describe differences.

- Use listing signals (*first, second, next, another, also,* etc.) to separate the differences.

Here are some common signal phrases you can use to draw contrasts. Notice the grammar and punctuation of each word and phrase.

Signal Words and Phrases	Examples
however, in contrast, on the other hand	Seattle has cool, rainy days all year long. **On the other hand**, Los Angeles has rain only in the fall and winter.
but	Seattle has cool, rainy days all year long, **but** Los Angeles has rain only in the fall and winter.
different	Mice and rats are **different** in several ways.
different from	Mice are **different from** rats.
unlike	**Unlike** mice, rats have small ears.

Practice 1

Read the outline for each paragraph of contrast. In each outline, underline all the sentences that support the topic sentence.

1 **Topic sentence:** If you want to fly to Boston, there are several differences between a NorthAir flight and a Friend Air flight.

The NorthAir flight is $120 cheaper than the Friend Air flight.

NorthAir has an on-time record of 88% on flights to Boston, but Friend Air's record is only 72%.

NorthAir planes have enough legroom for a tall person like me. In contrast, the seats on the Friend Air flight are crowded together.

Neither NorthAir nor Friend Air serve any food.

There is no checked baggage charge on NorthAir. However, Friend Air charges $35 per bag.

2 **Topic sentence:** In humans, there are a number of clear differences between male and female skeletons. The skeletal system provides support for the body.

Males have bigger, heavier bones than females.

Bones in the female body finish growing around age 18. On the other hand, bones in the male body continue to grow until age 21.

The bones of male and female babies are not very different.

In general, males have longer and heavier skulls than females.

Males have longer ribs than females. Also, male ribs are more curved than female ribs.

Human males and females have the same number of ribs.

3 **Topic sentence:** Asian elephants are different from African elephants in several ways.

African elephants have larger ears than Asian elephants.

An African elephant can weigh up to 7,500 kilograms. In contrast, the Asian elephant typically weighs about 6,000 kilograms.

African elephants are larger than Asian elephants. African males are about 4 meters tall; Asian males are about 3.5 meters tall.

On an African elephant, the highest point of the body is the shoulders. On an Asian elephant, the highest point is the back.

All African elephants have tusks, but only some male Asian elephants do.

Both African elephants and Asian elephants are mild-natured.

Practice 2

Read each paragraph of contrast. In each paragraph, underline one sentence that does not belong.

1 The two candidates for state senator from Croft County, Jerry Aspen and Carla Haigen, are different in several ways. To begin, they belong to different political parties. Jerry is a Democrat, but Carla is a Republican. Therefore, the candidates have different philosophies about taxes. They do have similar ideas about energy use and preventing pollution. Second, they have different backgrounds. Jerry was born in Croft County and comes from a family of farmers. Carla was born in Chicago and moved to Croft just eight years ago. Jerry and Carla also have different ideas about the future of Croft County. Unlike Carla, Jerry wants the county to stay rural, with a small population. Carla would like to attract more businesses to the county. Both Carla and Jerry are honest and hardworking politicians, but I plan to vote for Jerry Aspen because I agree with most of his ideas.

2 There are several basic differences between indoor volleyball and beach volleyball. The first and most obvious difference is that indoor volleyball is played indoors, on a court with wood floors, but beach volleyball is played outdoors on sand. Second, the sports are played with different numbers of players. In indoor volleyball there are six people on a team. In contrast, beach volleyball only has two players on a team. Next, the court sizes are different. Indoor volleyball courts measure 18-by-9-meters, but beach volleyball courts are smaller—16-by-8-meters. In addition, the two sports use different scoring systems. In indoor volleyball the first team to gain 25 points wins. In beach volleyball a game ends when one team reaches 21 points. Both sports use "rally" scoring, which means a team does not have to serve the ball to get a point.

Supporting Sentences
PROVIDING REASONS

Presentation

Providing Reasons

Reasons support your argument. They answer the question *why?* For example, you can use reasons to explain why you did something, decided something, or chose something.

When you give a list of reasons, you should use transitions to introduce each one. You should also use a transition to signal that you have reached the conclusion. Study the examples.

Transition Signals	Examples
Signaling reasons	*(reasons to explain why someone owns a motorcycle)* Pattern 1 **First of all,** a motorcycle is easy to park. **Second,** a motorcycle doesn't use much gas.
	Pattern 2 **The first reason is** the low cost. **Another reason is** the convenience.
	Pattern 3 The first reason **is that** it is easy to park. Another reason **is that** it doesn't use much gas.
Signaling the conclusion	**For these (three) reasons,** I decided to buy a motorcycle instead of a car. **Because of the low price and convenience,** I would rather own a motorcycle than a car.

Practice 1

Read the topic sentence and list of reasons. Underline the sentence that is not a reason.

1 Topic sentence: If you have only a few hours between flights, Amsterdam is the perfect city to visit.

The airport, Schiphol, is only 15 minutes from the city center.

There is a direct train between the airport and the city center.

The train leaves for the airport or the city center every ten minutes.

Amsterdam has excellent weather during the summer.

Amsterdam is small, so you can see a lot in the short time between your flights.

2 Topic sentence: I have decided to attend a community college for two years and then transfer to a four-year university.

There are three community colleges in my town.

By attending community college, I can live at home and save money.

The tuition at a community college is much lower than the tuition at a university.

Community colleges offer more night classes, so I can work during the daytime.

Community college classes cost less, so I can take many different classes before I choose my major.

Practice 2

Number each sentence in the correct order to form a paragraph supported by reasons.

Paragraph 1

_____ For all these reasons, I plan to get one or more pets as soon as I have my first child.

_____ A second reason to get a pet when children are small is that it teaches them responsibility. Even a three-year-old can help feed the dog or give water to the cat.

_____ There are several reasons why experts say it's good for small children to have pets.

_____ First of all, pets are fun to play with. Children can interact with living creatures instead of watching them passively on television.

_____ Finally, having pets is good for children's health. For example, research shows that owning a pet can help prevent allergies in children.

_____ Third, owning a pet teaches children to respect other living things.

Paragraph 2

_____ The first reason is that swimming is a vigorous sport. There is constant movement, which is good for the heart.

_____ All these reasons explain why I like swimming better than any other sport.

_____ There are four reasons why swimming is my favorite physical activity.

_____ A third reason why I enjoy swimming is that it feels good. I love the feeling of water on my skin. It feels cool and clean.

_____ The last reason I love swimming is the quiet. In the pool nobody is talking and there is no loud music playing. It's my favorite place to think.

_____ Second, swimming is good for flexibility. It is especially good for stretching the muscles of the back and shoulders. Because of swimming, I have never had any back or shoulder pain.

PROVIDING DETAILS

Copyright © 2017 by Pearson Education, Inc. Duplication is not permitted.

Presentation

Providing Details

- Details tell *who, what, when, where, why, how, how much, how many.*
- All the details in a paragraph must be related to the main idea stated in the topic sentence.
- Types of details include facts, statistics, examples, and reasons.

Type of Detail	Supporting Sentences
Fact	*(from a paragraph about the Fourth of July)* On the Fourth of July, Americans celebrate the birth of the United States in 1776.
Statistic	*(from a paragraph about Yosemite National Park)* Yosemite National Park covers an area of 761,268 acres.
Example	*(from a paragraph about teaching responsibility to children)* For example, children can be responsible for feeding pets and filling their water dishes.
Reasons	*(from a paragraph about hearing loss)* Listening to loud music with ear buds is one reason teenagers suffer hearing loss.

Practice 1

Read the topic sentence and supporting details. In each item, underline the detail that does not support the main idea of the paragraph.

1 **Topic sentence:** Antarctica is the coldest, windiest, and driest place on Earth.

The coldest temperature ever recorded on Earth—minus 89 degrees C—was recorded in Antarctica.

Wind speeds often reach 100 miles per hour.

Antarctica gets no rain and only about 2 inches of snow per year.

About 4,000 people visit Antarctica each year.

2 Topic sentence: Louis Braille (Jan. 4, 1809—Jan. 6, 1852) was the inventor of a system of raised dots used by blind people to read.

Louis Braille is buried in the Pantheon in Paris.

After losing his sight as a child, he invented his extraordinary system in his early teens.

In 1829, Braille published "The Method of Writing Words, Music, and Plain Song by Means of Dots, for Use by the Blind and Arranged by Them."

His method, called Braille, is still in use around the world today.

3 Topic sentence: My cousin Helen is one of the worst drivers I know.

She's always talking on her cell phone while she drives.

She rolls through stop signs instead of stopping completely.

She has an old, beat up Volkswagen Beetle.

She doesn't bother to use her turn signal when she's making a turn.

She drives with one hand and holds a cup of coffee in the other.

4 Topic sentence: I have decided to stop using credit cards for several reasons.

If I pay with a credit card, it's too easy for me to spend more money than I have.

Credit card companies charge 18% interest per month.

I got my first credit card when I was 18 years old.

It's easy to get into debt if you don't pay off your balance each month.

If someone steals your credit card, he or she can buy expensive things in your name.

5 Topic sentence: Cats make wonderful pets.

They are quiet, beautiful, and extremely clean.

Unlike dogs, cats like being left alone.

Some people are allergic to cats.

Most cats are loving and friendly.

I enjoy watching television with my cat on my lap.

Practice 2

Read the topic sentence. In each item, underline three details that provide good support.

1 Topic sentence: Broccoli is one of the healthiest vegetables you can eat.

One cup of broccoli contains all the vitamin C you need in a day to help you stay healthy.

Broccoli has lots of fiber to help your digestive system work properly.

Broccoli is a plant in the cabbage family.

Broccoli contains glucoraphanin, which helps the body to fight cancer.

Some people say that broccoli doesn't taste good.

2 Topic sentence: Greeting customs differ widely from culture to culture.

Americans are quick to use people's first names.

In North America, greetings usually involve some form of touching—a handshake, a hug, or a kiss.

When Thai people say hello, they press their hands together at chest level and bow their heads slightly.

It is offensive to touch a person's head in Thailand.

In Japan, it is traditional for people to bow when they meet and greet each other.

3 Topic sentence: Kangaroos are social animals that live in large family groups called "mobs."

A mob can have as many as 100 kangaroos.

Kangaroos are mammals.

The head of the mob is the largest male in the group, called a "boomer" or "old man."

There are 47 species of kangaroos.

Living in a group offers protection for younger and weaker animals.

GIVING EXAMPLES

Giving Examples

Examples are a common type of supporting detail. Examples can support the topic sentence directly, or they can support a major sub-point of the topic sentence. For example:

Topic sentence: My friend Ari enjoys every kind of outdoor sport.

Example: For example, he loves playing basketball with his friends.

Topic sentence: My friend Susanna can cook almost any kind of ethnic food.

Sub-point: First of all, she makes excellent Mexican food.

Example: For example, she knows how to prepare delicious fish tacos.

Use the transitions *for example*, *for instance*, and *such as* to introduce examples.

- *For example* and *for instance* are the same. You can put them at the beginning of a sentence or in the middle.
- *Such as* can only go in the middle of a sentence.

Notice the use of commas with these transitions.

Transitions	Examples
for example, for instance	I wear different kinds of shoes for different purposes. **For example,** I wear running shoes for jogging.
	A number of famous singers are blind. Stevie Wonder, **for instance,** has been blind since the day he was born.
such as	I read an article about unusual fruits **such as** durian, paw paw, and citron.
	A number of fruits, **such as** durian, paw paw, and citron, are not common in the United States.

Practice 1

Draw lines to match the general statements on the left to the specific examples on the right.

My grandmother never wastes anything.

Dorian has several interesting hobbies.

Honeybees communicate the location of food by dancing.

2011 was a year of amazing scientific discoveries.

In recent years, my city's newspaper has changed in many ways.

In my city, the weather can be very unpredictable in June.

I have a special drawer where I keep my "treasures."

Several human foods are toxic to dogs.

My sister doesn't look like anyone else in the family.

Different kinds of wood are useful for different purposes.

For example, she has blond hair and blue eyes, but the rest of us have dark hair and brown eyes.

For instance, the temperature can go up or down by 20 degrees in one day.

For instance, scientists at Oxford University developed the first vaccine against malaria.

Fruits, such as grapes and raisins, can lead to kidney failure in dogs.

For example, it no longer has a weekly health section.

Oak, for example, is useful for making strong furniture like dining tables because it is very heavy.

A movement called the "waggle dance," for example, indicates that food is far away.

For example, she goes to a belly dancing class once a week.

For example, this drawer is where I keep letters from my grandfather.

For instance, she washes and reuses plastic bags.

Practice 2

Write the sentence parts and transitions as sentences. Keep the phrases in the same order. Pay attention to commas and capital letters.

1 My cat likes to eat vegetables / for example / she loves tomatoes.

My cat likes to eat vegetables. _____

2 British singer Adele can sing in many different styles / for instance/ she is famous as a soul singer.

British singer Adele can sing in many different styles. _____

3 There are several all-electric cars on the market / such as / the Nissan Leaf and the Chevy Volt.

There are several all-electric cars on the market, _____.

4 Paul has unusual eating habits / for example / he eats leftover pizza for breakfast.

Paul has unusual eating habits. _____

5 My new phone has many amazing features / for instance / it can tell me the weather in any city.

My new phone has many amazing features. _____

6 Bacteria are essential for good health / for example / they are necessary for proper digestion.

Bacteria are essential for good health. _____

7 There are many differences in vocabulary between British and American English. An elevator / for instance / is called a lift in Britain.

There are many differences in vocabulary between British and American English. _____

8 Many electrical devices are smaller than they used to be. Personal computers / for example / weighed 40 pounds at one time.

Many electrical devices are smaller than they used to be.

_____

9 The United States exports enormous quantities of grains / such as / wheat, corn, and soybeans.

The United States exports enormous quantities of grains, _____.

10 My sister is very sensitive to loud noises / for example / loud car horns make her nervous.

My sister is very sensitive to loud noises. _____

11 My friend Tracy is one of the kindest people I know / for instance / she volunteers at a children's hospital every Saturday.

My friend Tracy is one of the kindest people I know. _____

EXPRESSING OPINIONS

Expressing Opinions

An opinion is a belief. Opinions are different from facts. Facts are true statements that can be checked. You can disagree with an opinion, but you cannot disagree with a fact.

In an opinion paragraph, your purpose is to persuade people to agree with you, to take action, or to change their behavior. An opinion paragraph has these parts:

- **Topic sentence:** This sentence states the topic and your opinion about it.

- **Supporting sentences:** These sentences give reasons to support your opinion. List your reasons and include facts or examples to support each one.

- **Concluding sentence:** Restate your opinion, remind your reader of your reasons, or, if you like, give advice using the words *should* or *should not*.

You can use these signal words and phrases in an opinion paragraph:

Signal Words and Phrases	Examples
To state your opinion I think . . .	**I believe** it should be illegal for private citizens to own guns.
I believe . . .	
In my opinion,	**In my opinion,** high school students should be required to study at least two years of a foreign language.
I am for / against . . .	
To connect reasons The (My) first (second) reason is that . . .	**My first reason is that** many people die in accidental shootings every year. Another reason is that . . .
First of all, Second, etc.	
The final reason is . . .	
Finally,	
Last,	
To signal the conclusion For (all) these reasons . . .	**For these three reasons,** I believe Jane Jackson is the best candidate for mayor of Smalltown.
These reasons explain why . . .	**These reasons explain why** I think there should be a tax on soft drinks and artificial fruit drinks.

Practice 1

In each outline, underline three reasons that support the opinion in the topic sentence.

Paragraph 1

Topic sentence: Some parents believe that spanking is an effective way to discipline children, but I think spanking is very harmful to children.

Spanking teaches children that it is OK to hit someone if you don't like what they are doing.

Spanking is painful and cruel.

Spanking is a normal form of discipline in many cultures.

When I was a child, my mother spanked me if I was rude.

Spanking does not teach children how to correct their behavior.

Spanking harms parents by making them feel like bullies.

Paragraph 2

Topic sentence: I believe public schools should offer art education to children for three reasons.

Parents, not public schools, should pay for children to learn music, drawing, dance, and other arts.

According to research, art helps children develop every part of their brains.

Art helps children learn academic skills. For example, music and drawing can help students learn mathematics.

Because of budget problems, schools all over the country have cut classes in art and sports.

Children who are not good at traditional subjects may develop confidence by participating in art activities.

However, I think it's a bad idea to give children grades on their art projects.

Practice 2

Number each sentence in the correct order to form a paragraph of opinion. Some of them have been done for you.

Paragraph 1

_____ First of all, writing in my journal helps me develop fluency.

_____ Second, when I write in my journal, I can practice using new vocabulary I've learned.

_____ These reasons explain why keeping a journal has really helped my English. If you want to improve your English skills, why don't you try it?

___1__ I believe that keeping a journal is an excellent way for me to improve my English.

_____ In addition, writing in my journal helps me see my progress in English.

_____ For example, last week I learned the word "determination" in my English class. Last night, I used that word in my journal.

___3__ I can write without stopping because I don't have to worry about making mistakes.

Paragraph 2

___3__ If a customer with a dog comes into a store, those people might feel they need to leave out of fear. It isn't fair to them.

_____ I love dogs, but for these reasons, I believe people should leave their dogs at home when they visit public buildings.

_____ For example, some dogs don't like children. If a child tries to pet a dog in a department store, the dog might bite the child.

_____ Third, dogs may use the floor as a toilet.

___1__ In my opinion, people should not be allowed to bring dogs into public buildings like department stores and restaurants.

_____ Finally, dogs can be noisy. Nobody wants to hear a dog barking when they're shopping or eating out.

_____ Secondly, dogs can be dangerous.

_____ Imagine that you're eating in a restaurant, and a dog urinates under the table next to you. This happened to me last week.

_____ First, many people are afraid of dogs.

The Conclusion

Presentation

The Conclusion

Paragraphs usually have a concluding sentence. This sentence signals that your paragraph is finished. A well-written concluding sentence has one or more of the following characteristics:

- It does not include any new information about the topic.
- It restates the topic sentence in a different way.
- It summarizes the main points.
- It presents the writer's opinion or final thoughts about the topic.

Concluding sentences often begin with a transitional phrase such as *In brief, In short, In conclusion, To conclude, In summary, To summarize,* or *To sum up.* Each phrase is followed by a comma.

Example:

In short, the speaker fails to show how watching television is healthy.

In conclusion, we must reject his call for a television in every household.

Practice 1

Read the topic sentence and supporting points. Circle the letter next to the best concluding sentence.

Example:

1 Topic sentence: *Since it is convenient, inexpensive, and relaxing, I usually take the train to work instead of driving.*

Supporting points:
- *The train station is a five-minute walk from my apartment.*
- *A train ticket costs much less than parking downtown.*
- *I can read, talk to people, or watch the scenery.*

a *On the other hand, the train is very crowded during the afternoon rush hour.*
b *In conclusion, I have met many interesting people on the train to and from work.*
(c) *To sum up, these three advantages explain why I would rather take the train to work than drive my car.*

2 Topic sentence: There are a number of good reasons to rent an apartment instead of buying your own home.

Supporting points:

- If you decide to move to a new area or city, you can easily pack up and leave.
- It is not your responsibility to fix things that break.
- An apartment is easier to clean than a house.

a In short, these reasons explain why many people would rather rent an apartment than buy a home.

b In summary, renting an apartment is cheaper than buying a home.

c In conclusion, I'm sure you can understand why most Americans still dream of buying their own home.

3 Topic sentence: Recent research suggests that drinking coffee may be good for people's health.

Supporting points:

- It helps to prevent type 2 diabetes.
- It seems to lower the risk of some types of cancer.
- It helps lower depression in some people.
- It helps people concentrate.

a In addition, nothing tastes better than a cup of coffee in the morning.

b On the other hand, the caffeine in coffee makes some people nervous.

c So enjoy your morning cup of coffee—it's good for you!

Practice 2

Read the paragraph. Circle the number next to the best description of the concluding sentence.

1 Like most people from my country, Lebanon, I love hummus. Hummus is one of the most popular foods in the Middle East. It is served as an appetizer or side dish at almost every meal. Hummus is made from ground chickpeas (also called garbanzo beans). It is mixed with olive oil, garlic, and lemon juice to form a thick paste. We eat hummus with a special type of bread called pita. We tear off a piece of pita and use it to scoop up some hummus. We can also put the hummus inside the pita along with salad, grilled vegetables, or meat and eat it like a sandwich. Hummus is very delicious and very nutritious as well. In short, if you ever come to my country, I hope you will try hummus.

The concluding sentence:

a restates the topic sentence

b summarizes the main points

c presents the writer's opinion or final thoughts

2 Cockroaches have lived on Earth for more than 400 million years. Three characteristics explain this insect's amazing ability to survive. First of all, cockroaches can live almost anywhere—outdoors in tropical climates and indoors in cooler ones. They prefer warm, humid places; therefore, they are often found in homes and factories where food is prepared and stored. Another characteristic that helps cockroaches survive is that they will eat almost anything. Their diet includes not only human food but also dead insects, paper, and even glue! Finally, cockroaches have few natural enemies. They smell bad, and eating them causes most birds and animals to get sick. These characteristics explain why cockroaches have existed longer than almost any other creature on Earth.
The concluding sentence:
a restates the topic sentence
b summarizes the main points
c presents the writer's opinion or final thoughts

3 People who immigrate to Los Angeles come to the city for three main reasons. The first is the city's dry, sunny climate. It does not rain much, so people can enjoy outdoor activities year round. People also come to Los Angeles because there are many job opportunities here. Los Angeles is the business, financial, and, of course, entertainment capital of the United States. The movie industry alone employs many thousands of people per year. Finally, many people come to Los Angeles because of its great diversity of people. There are dozens of different ethnic groups here, such as Koreans, Russians, Iranians, Ethiopians, Armenians, and many more. Each group contributes to the city's culture. For example, you can find almost any type of food in Los Angeles. In brief, the city's weather, economic opportunities, and diversity explain why Los Angeles is such an attractive place to live.
The concluding sentence:
a restates the topic sentence
b summarizes the main points
c presents the writer's opinion or final thoughts

Unity

Presentation

Paragraph Unity

Good paragraphs have **unity**. This means all the sentences in the paragraph are about the same main idea. To check your writing for unity, ask yourself these questions:

- What is my topic?
- What is my controlling idea?
- Do all the supporting sentences in my paragraph talk about this topic and this controlling idea?

Example:

In this example, the underlined sentence does not belong. It's not related to the topic of the paragraph (protect your skin) or the controlling idea (steps).

> If you have light skin and light eyes, you need to take special steps to protect your skin from the sun. First, you should always wear sunscreen outdoors, even if the sun is not shining. Be sure to re-apply it every two hours. Next, wear a hat because you can get sunburned under your hair. <u>My grandfather never wore a hat and he got skin cancer.</u> Third, wear a long-sleeved shirt and long pants. These steps may be inconvenient, but they are necessary in order to keep your skin healthy and young looking.

Practice 1

Read each paragraph. Then read the list of sentences. Underline two sentences that will make a unified paragraph.

1 Working in my garden is enjoyable and helps me stay healthy. First, I get a lot of pleasure from working in my garden. I love putting plants in the ground, taking care of them, and watching them grow. When I work in my garden, I enjoy talking to people who walk by with their dogs or their children. Finally, gardening is excellent exercise. For all these reasons I try to spend at least an hour every day working in my garden.

If I plant seeds, I always get excited when the first bits of green appear above the ground.

Carrying pots and bags of fertilizer keeps my muscles strong.

All my neighbors are very friendly.

2 My grandmother is 92 years old, but she is still mentally and physically active. To exercise her mind, my grandmother reads, plays word games, and watches movies in French. To stay physically fit, she swims and walks every day. In addition, my grandmother has a young spirit. In short, my grandmother loves life, and that's why I love spending time with her.

My grandmother was born in New York City in 1920.

She still cleans her house all by herself.

She knows how to use a computer and enjoys writing emails to all her family members.

3 You can save water by following some or all of these easy tips. Inside the house, be sure to fix dripping faucets. Take short showers. Outside the house, water plants only in the early morning when it's cool. If possible, replace your lawn with low-water plants.

Don't leave water running while you brush your teeth.

Get a large container and use it to collect rainwater.

Don't ask for clean towels every day if you're staying at a hotel.

Practice 2

In each paragraph, underline one sentence that does not belong.

1 Living in your own apartment after college has two big advantages. First, you can have privacy. You can choose when to be alone and when to be with people. You can listen to the music and watch the television programs you like. I like watching reality shows like "Lost." Second, living in your own apartment teaches you responsibility. You have to remember to pay the rent and electricity. You have to clean and cook your own food. If you don't do these things, nobody will do them for you. For these reasons, I am really looking forward to living in my own apartment after I graduate.

2 Corn is native to North and South America. The Indians grew corn here for thousands of years before Columbus arrived. Today you can see fossils of ancient corn in museums. When Columbus and his ships landed in the Caribbean in 1492, he traded with the natives and took corn back to Spain. From there, corn was introduced to other European countries and, later, to the rest of the world.

3 Online courses are a convenient and easy way for some students to take college courses. First of all, online courses have flexible schedules. You can go online and do your work whenever you choose. This is very convenient for people who have jobs or young children. The second advantage of online courses is that they are efficient. You can learn at your own speed. For example, you can stop and check a dictionary when you don't understand something. You need a computer in order to take online classes. These are two reasons why I like taking online courses.

WRITING ASSIGNMENTS

Paragraph

DESCRIBING PEOPLE

> **Presentation**
>
> **Model Paragraph**
>
> **My Neighbor Peter**
>
> Of all the people in my neighborhood, the person I like the most is my neighbor Peter. He is 25 years old. He's tall and thin, and he has long black hair and brown eyes. He always wears casual clothes, like T-shirts and jeans. I like him for several reasons. First, he's very friendly. When I moved into the neighborhood last year, he came over and introduced himself. We became friends very quickly. He has a great sense of humor, too. He tells very funny jokes and always makes me laugh. Peter is also an interesting person. He has an unusual job. He's a drummer in a jazz band. The people in his band sometimes come to his house to practice there. I like to listen to them practice. Last month, Peter and his band played a show at a local club, and I went. They were great! Another reason I like Peter is that he is generous. Before I met him, I didn't know anything about jazz music, but he has taught me a lot. He often lets me borrow his CDs. I think that I am lucky to have such a friendly, funny, interesting, and generous neighbor. I'm glad he is also my friend.

Write a paragraph about one of the topics listed below (or the topic your teacher assigns). You will have 50 minutes.

1 Introduce yourself by describing what you look like, your personality, and what you like to do.

2 Think about a friend or family member. Describe what that person is like and what he or she is doing right now.

3 Choose a famous person you are familiar with. Describe what this person does, what he or she is like, and your opinion of this person.

Editing Checklist

Are the grammar, sentence structure, mechanics, and punctuation correct?

Is the vocabulary appropriate? Are the words spelled correctly?

Is the paragraph well organized, well developed, and clear?

Describing People

The key to writing a good descriptive paragraph is to include details that will help the reader form a picture of the person you are describing.

A paragraph describing a person should include these parts:

A topic sentence: Introduce the person you are describing. Give the person's name and make a general statement about him or her. (Example: Of all the people in my neighborhood, the person I like the most is my neighbor Peter.)

Supporting sentences: Include several sentences about the person's appearance (weight, height, age, body type, hair, eyes, features), style, talents, or behavior. Include descriptive words and examples that "paint a picture" of the person.

A concluding sentence: Summarize the person's characteristics. Then say how you feel about the person. (Example: I think that I am lucky to have such a friendly, funny, interesting, and generous neighbor. I'm glad he is also my friend.)

_____

_____

_____

_____

_____

_____

_____

_____

_____

_____

_____

_____

_____

_____

COMPARING AND CONTRASTING

Model Paragraph

My Offices

I have two offices for my job, and they are very different from each other. One office is at my home, and the other one is at the school where I teach. My office at home is comfortable. There's a sofa across from my desk, and I can relax on it when I need to take a break. The office has a big window, so I can enjoy the sunshine as I work. The light helps me to stay awake and feel refreshed. My home office also looks good. There are interesting pictures on the walls, and the carpet is new. Also, because I work alone there, I can play music when I'm working. I love to work in my home office. On the other hand, my office at school is not as comfortable. I have my own desk and chair, but there's no sofa in the room. There's a window, but it's very small, and I can't even see it from my desk. This office doesn't look as good as my home office, either. The walls need paint, and the carpet is old. Also, because a lot of teachers work there with me, I can't play music whenever I want. In short, my two offices are very different, and I definitely prefer working at my home office. It's more comfortable, it looks nicer, and I feel happier there.

Write a paragraph about one of the topics listed below (or the topic your teacher assigns). You will have 50 minutes.

1 Compare two movies. Explain how they are similar or different.

2 Compare two family members. Explain how their appearance and personalities are similar or different.

3 Compare two cities you are familiar with. Explain how they are similar or different.

Editing Checklist

Are the grammar, sentence structure, mechanics, and punctuation correct?

Is the vocabulary appropriate? Are the words spelled correctly?

Is the paragraph well organized, well developed, and clear?

Comparing and Contrasting

Very often in our writing we need to explain how two things are similar or different. "Compare" means to focus on similarities. "Contrast" means to focus on differences. Some paragraphs are only about similarities, some are only about differences, and some combine both types of details.

A paragraph of comparison or contrast should include these parts:

The topic sentence: Your topic sentence should name the two people, things, or places you are comparing. It should also indicate the focus of your paragraph: similarities, differences, or both. (Example: I have two offices for my job, and they are very different from one another.)

Supporting sentences: The simplest way to organize a comparison and contrast paragraph is in two "blocks." Explain or describe your first item. Write a transition, and then explain or describe how the second item is similar to or different from the first one. Here is a sample outline of a paragraph organized in two blocks:

I Topic sentence: I have two offices for my job, and they are very different from one another.

a. My home office

    1. Comfort

    2. Appearance

    3. I can play music

Transition: On the other hand

b. My work office

    1. Comfort

    2. Appearance

    3. I can't play music

The concluding sentence: There are many ways to conclude a comparison/contrast paragraph. One way is to summarize the similarities or differences and then to add a final thought. For example, if you are comparing two things, you can say which one you like better.

There are many expressions you can use to talk about similarities and differences. Here are a few:

Similarities: like / alike / similar to / also, too / both… and / the same

Differences: difference / different (from) / in contrast / on the other hand / but

DESCRIBING AN EVENT

Presentation

Model Paragraph

My First Time Kayaking

I'll never forget the first time I went kayaking. Ten years ago, I traveled to Poland with a group of Americans. We decided to rent kayaks (small, two-person boats) for a weekend trip down a local river. At first, we were very excited. The sun was shining and the river was sparkling. We jumped in our kayaks and started to paddle. Many of us weren't sure how to paddle correctly, but my friend Matt taught us how to do it. It was easy. As we went down the river, we sang songs and told funny stories. However, after about two hours, clouds covered the sun. Small raindrops started to fall. We thought it was no problem, but then the rain got harder and harder. Soon, it was raining very hard, and we had to stop under a bridge. We ate lunch in our boats under the bridge and waited for the rain to stop. But it didn't stop. In fact, the rain did not stop for two whole days. We had no choice. We had to keep going. We kayaked down the river in the pouring rain for two days, and we camped at night in the rain, too. By the end of the trip, we were extremely wet, cold, and tired. I was so happy to put on a sweater, eat some hot soup and go to sleep in a hotel! That trip was very difficult, but it helped me discover that I love kayaking. Now, I have my own kayak and go on a lot of river trips, but only when it's not raining.

Write a paragraph about one of the topics listed below (or the topic your teacher assigns). You will have 50 minutes.

Editing Checklist

- Are the grammar, sentence structure, mechanics, and punctuation correct?
- Is the vocabulary appropriate? Are the words spelled correctly?
- Is the paragraph well organized, well developed, and clear?

Describing an Event or Series of Events

To describe an event or a series of events, you will need to write your paragraph in time order. That means you begin with the earliest event and finish with the last one. You can write about something that happened to you, to another person, or to a place.

A paragraph about an event should include these parts:

The topic sentence: In this sentence you should introduce the event and make a statement that will motivate your readers to keep reading. Your topic sentence should make the reader ask, "What happened next"?

The supporting sentences: Describe the events in the order that they happened. Use time order signals like these:

Transitions

Examples: first, second, next, later, after that, finally

i.e.: I had a wonderful time at my 20th birthday party. First, my girlfriend picked me up in her car and….

Dates and times

Examples: On May 4, in the morning, two weeks ago, today, before breakfast, at 8:00 a.m.

i.e.: Natalie Portman, the famous actress, has had a very interesting life. She was born in Jerusalem, Israel, on June 9, 1981.

The concluding sentence: Write a final comment about the experience. For example, tell if it was good or bad. You can also say what you learned or how you changed after this experience.

1 Tell the story of an event you remember from your childhood.

2 Describe a wedding or other ceremony that you attended in the past.

3 Tell the life story of a family member.

4 Tell the life story of a famous person you are familiar with.

SUPPORTING AN OPINION

Presentation

Model Paragraph

No Pets on Airplanes

In my opinion, people should not be allowed to bring pets on airplanes. I have several reasons for my opinion. First, many people are allergic to cats or dogs. If they are sitting near someone's pet on a crowded flight, it might not be possible for them to move to a different seat. They could get sick. Second, pets may disturb human passengers. Dogs in particular can be noisy. They may bark and upset passengers who are trying to read, sleep, or just relax. Third, a pet may escape from its carrier and create a dangerous situation in the plane. One time I was flying to Los Angeles, and a woman took her cat out of its carrier. Well, the cat jumped out of her arms and began running around the plane. I think it was terrified and wanted to find a place to hide. Instead of helping passengers, the flight attendants had to spend time trying to catch the cat. This created an unsafe situation. In summary, these reasons explain why I don't think pets should be allowed to fly as passengers in airplanes. I think airlines should require all animals to fly in the cargo area of the plane.

Write a paragraph about one of the topics listed below (or the topic your teacher assigns). You will have 50 minutes.

1 State your opinion on smoking in public places. Support your ideas with reasons and examples.

2 State your opinion on how to reduce crime. Support your ideas with reasons and examples.

3 State your opinion on an issue in the news. Support your ideas with reasons and examples.

Editing Checklist

Are the grammar, sentence structure, mechanics, and punctuation correct?

Is the vocabulary appropriate? Are the words spelled correctly?

Is the paragraph well organized, well developed, and clear?

Supporting an Opinion

Sometimes it is necessary to give your opinion when you write. Your goal in this kind of writing is to persuade people to agree with you, to take action, or to change a behavior. After you state your opinion, you should support it with facts, examples, and reasons.

A paragraph of opinion should include these parts:

A topic sentence: In an opinion paragraph, this sentence states the topic and your opinion about it. (Example: In my opinion, people should not be allowed to bring pets on airplanes.)

Supporting sentences: These sentences give facts, examples, and reasons that support your opinion. (Examples: Many people are allergic to dogs or cats. Pets may disturb human passengers. A pet may escape from its carrier and create a dangerous situation in the plane.)

A **concluding sentence:** This sentence summarizes the main points in the paragraph or adds a final comment. (Example: In summary, these reasons explain why I don't think pets should be allowed to fly as passengers in airplanes.)

You can use these expressions to state your opinion:

I think…

I believe…

In my opinion, …

I am against…

GIVING INSTRUCTIONS

Model Paragraph

How to Pack for a Camping Trip

Packing for a camping trip in the mountains is easy if you follow these steps. First, check your equipment. Make sure your tent, sleeping bag, camp stove, and flashlights are in good condition. Before you go on your trip, practice putting up your tent and using your camp stove. That way, you won't have any problems when you get to your campsite. Second, pack the right clothes. Check the weather before you go, and make sure to bring warm clothes like long underwear, socks, and a wool hat. Bring a rain poncho with a hood since it may rain. Don't bring cotton clothes. If they get wet, they stay wet for a long time. Next, be organized when you pack. Divide your things into a lot of small cloth bags. You can even put clothes in one of them and use it as a pillow, and then you won't need to carry an extra pillow with you. Finally, plan your food and water. The day before the trip, make a trail mix of raisins, peanuts, chocolate, and dried fruit. Bring things that are easy to cook on a camp stove, like instant rice, beans, oats, and pasta. You should also go to a camping store and buy special tablets to clean your drinking water. This way, you don't have to carry a lot of water with you. In summary, if you follow these instructions and spend the time to prepare well, you will have an enjoyable camping trip with no unpleasant surprises.

Write a paragraph about one of the topics listed below (or the topic your teacher assigns). You will have 50 minutes.

1 Give instructions on how to be well prepared to take a test.

2 Give instructions for how to prepare to go through security at the airport before a flight.

3 Give instructions for how to behave when visiting another country.

Editing Checklist

Are the grammar, sentence structure, mechanics, and punctuation correct?

Is the vocabulary appropriate? Are the words spelled correctly?

Is the paragraph well organized, well developed, and clear?

Giving Instructions

Paragraphs that give instructions are sometimes called "how to" paragraphs because they explain how to do or make something.

An instruction paragraph should include these parts:

The topic sentence: The topic sentence should name the topic and say that the paragraph will give instructions about it. Key words to include in the topic sentence are steps, instructions, advice, process. For example:

To make a delicious bean dip for chips, follow these easy steps.

You can avoid jet lag when travelling overseas if you follow my advice.

Supporting sentences: Divide the instructions into a list of steps or suggestions. Name each one. Then explain each of them in one or two sentences. Introduce each new step with transitions such as *first*, *second*, *also*, *in addition*, and *finally*.

Use the command form of verbs to give instructions. For example:

Check your equipment before you leave.

Don't pack cotton clothes.

A concluding sentence: Restate or refer back to the topic sentence and state what positive result will happen if the reader follows the steps you have described.

_____

_____

_____

_____

_____

_____

_____

_____

_____

_____

_____

_____

_____

_____

_____

_____

_____

_____

_____

DESCRIBING A PLACE

Model Paragraph

The Public Park

The public park near my house is a great place to relax and have fun. It has many enjoyable features. When you enter the park, on your left you will see two volleyball nets set up on the grass. Behind the volleyball nets, there is a beautiful blue swimming pool surrounded by a tall fence. In the summer, it is usually full of people in brightly colored swimsuits laughing, splashing, and swimming. Next to the pool on the right side, there is a colorful new playground. It is busy all the time with lots of energetic children. In the middle of the playground, there is a structure that looks like a big mushroom. On hot days, it sprays water into the air to keep everybody cool. Behind the playground, there is a big green soccer field. A jogging track goes all around the field. On the track, you can see people walking, jogging, and even riding bicycles. To the right of the soccer field, there are outdoor basketball courts that are always in use. You can hear the sound of the basketballs bouncing on the pavement and the laughing and shouting of the players. Finally, in between all these places, there are grassy areas with picnic tables, grills for cooking, and shady trees. You can see people relaxing on blankets in the grass, and you can smell meat cooking on the grill. I love to spend time at the park. It is an enjoyable, relaxing place.

Write a paragraph about one of the topics listed below (or the topic your teacher assigns). You will have 50 minutes.

1 Describe your country, its geography, and its most important regions and cities.

2 Describe a classroom at your school, explaining where everything is located in the room.

3 Describe the inside of a museum, mall, theater, or other building you are familiar with, explaining where things are located and what the building looks like inside.

Editing Checklist

Are the grammar, sentence structure, mechanics, and punctuation correct?

Is the vocabulary appropriate? Are the words spelled correctly?

Is the paragraph well organized, well developed, and clear?

Describing a Place

When you describe a place, you tell what it looks like and where things in it are located. There are two keys to writing a good description of a place:

use space order

use lots of adjectives and colorful details

A paragraph describing a place should include these parts:

The topic sentence: The topic sentence should name the place you are going to describe. Then it should make a general statement about the place. For example: "The public park near my house is a great place to relax and have fun."

Supporting sentences: These sentences provide details about what the place looks like and how the items in it are organized. Here are some of the ways that you can organize these details:

left to right or right to left

front to back or back to front

top to bottom or bottom to top

inside to outside or outside to inside

near to far or far to near

clockwise or counter-clockwise

Connect the locations with prepositionnal phrases. For example: *on the right, next to the _____, in front of the _____, by the _____,* and so on.

The concluding sentence: This sentence may repeat the general statement you made in your topic sentence. However, it should use different words. For example: "I love spending time in the park near my house. It's an enjoyable, relaxing place."

_____

_____

_____

_____

_____

_____

_____

_____

_____

_____

_____

_____

_____

LISTING QUALITIES

Model Paragraph

What's a Good Hairstylist?

Good hairstylists have four important characteristics. First of all, they need to have excellent training. Because hair fashions change all the time, skilled stylists take the time to learn about modern styles and haircutting methods. Second, good hairstylists know how to listen to their customers. They pay close attention to what their customers say they want and don't want. If customers aren't sure or don't know how to communicate clearly, good stylists will ask questions or show photos to help customers decide. In addition, good hairstylists take their time. They work slowly in order to avoid mistakes. One of the biggest mistakes is cutting hair too short. Stylists who work slowly and carefully make sure this mistake does not happen. Finally, good hairstylists are friendly and outgoing. They know how to make their customers feel comfortable by starting interesting conversations with them. This can help nervous customers feel relaxed and confident. In summary, if you look for a hairstylist who is well-trained, good at listening, careful, and friendly, you will probably be very pleased with the haircut you receive.

Write a paragraph about one of the topics listed below (or the topic your teacher assigns). You will have 50 minutes.

1 Describe three or four characteristics of a successful businessperson.

2 Describe several advantages or disadvantages of living in a large city.

3 Describe several different kinds of drivers.

Editing Checklist

Are the grammar, sentence structure, mechanics, and punctuation correct?

Is the vocabulary appropriate? Are the words spelled correctly?

Is the paragraph well organized, well developed, and clear?

Listing Qualities

Listing order is used very often in English. In this type of organization, you select a topic and a specific focus for developing the topic (known as a **controlling idea**). You then divide the focus into a number of separate points such as characteristics, types, benefits, reasons, and so on.

A listing-order paragraph should include these parts:

The topic sentence: The topic sentence should name the topic and the controlling idea and state how you will divide it into sections. For example:

A city bus driver needs to have three important qualities.

There are three benefits to having a parrot as a pet.

Olympic sports can be divided into two groups: team sports and individual sports.

Supporting sentences: Name each point and explain it in one or two sentences. Separate the points with listing-order transitions such as *first*, *second*, *next*, *in addition*, and *finally*.

The concluding sentence: Restate or summarize the points you listed, and add a memorable final statement.

Following are some common ways of dividing listing-order paragraphs: characteristics / qualities / advantages (benefits) / disadvantages

types / kinds / ways, methods / systems

_____

_____

_____

_____

_____

_____

_____

_____

_____

_____

_____

_____

_____

_____

_____

_____

_____

_____

EXPLAINING CAUSES

Presentation

Model Paragraph

Obesity

There are several reasons why millions of people are overweight nowadays. First, many people don't exercise enough. They often have to sit in front of a computer all day at work. Then they come home and choose to sit in front of the TV all evening. Because people sit too much without exercising, they get fat. In addition, people often eat a lot of fast food. Maybe they don't have a lot of time to cook healthy meals, so they go to fast food restaurants. People also like fast food since it is very cheap. However, fast food is full of fat and salt, so it makes people gain weight quickly. Another reason why people are overweight is because they drink too much soda. According to nutritionists, one can of soda has as much sugar as a candy bar. Many people drink several cans of soda each day, and all that sugar can make them fat and unhealthy. If people exercise, eat healthy food, and drink water instead of soda, they will become thinner and healthier.

Write a paragraph about one of the topics listed below (or the topic your teacher assigns). You will have 50 minutes.

Editing Checklist

- Are the grammar, sentence structure, mechanics, and punctuation correct?
- Is the vocabulary appropriate? Are the words spelled correctly?
- Is the paragraph well organized, well developed, and clear?

Writing about Causes

When you write about why you did something or why something happened, you are writing about causes. Causes are the same as reasons.

A paragraph about causes should include these parts:

A topic sentence: Include the situation (what happened or what you did and the number of causes. You can use expressions like *several reasons, two important causes, three major reasons*, etc.

Supporting sentences: List each reason and include one or more sentences to explain it. Separate the reasons with listing signals such as *The first reason, the second cause, next, third,* and *finally*.

A concluding sentence: Summarize your reasons and restate or refer back to your topic sentence. Use phrases such as *These three reasons explain why …, For these reasons, …,* and *Now you understand why…*.

Use these signal words and phrases to talk about causes.

Because + clause, i.e.: Because the temperature was below zero, the car would not start.

since + **clause,** i.e.: We stayed home since the buses were not running.

due to + **noun phrase,** i.e.: Due to his son's illness, Mr. Smith stayed home from work.

because of + **noun phrase,** i.e.: We stayed home because of the terrible weather.

1 Describe the causes of pollution.

2 Describe what causes young people to drop out of school.

3 Describe the causes of crime.

EXPLAINING EFFECTS

Presentation

Model Paragraph

My Money Problems

My city's money problems are causing some problems in my life. First of all, I am worried about losing my job as a librarian. Because of the budget problems, public services like parks and libraries don't have enough money to operate. Many city employees have lost their jobs, and I am afraid that I might be next. The shortage of money is also having an effect on our schools. For example, most public schools don't offer art and music classes anymore. My son's school cut all its art classes, so now I have to pay for expensive private art lessons for him. I worry that I won't be able to pay for them if I lose my job. Finally, the city's money problems are hurting our transportation system. Buses and subways do not come as often as they did in the past. Because I take the bus to work every day, that makes my life more inconvenient. It takes me a very long time to get to work. Also, I often don't get a seat on the bus since it's so crowded. Therefore, I am usually tired when I arrive at work, and sometimes I'm late. In summary, my city's money troubles are creating serious problems for me and my family. If the situation doesn't improve, we may have to move to another city.

Write a paragraph about one of the topics listed below (or the topic your teacher assigns). You will have 50 minutes.

1 Describe the effects pollution has on people and animals.

2 Many young people drop out of school each year. Describe the effects dropping out of school has on young people's lives.

3 Describe the effects crime has on people's lives.

Editing Checklist

Are the grammar, sentence structure, mechanics, and punctuation correct?

Is the vocabulary appropriate? Are the words spelled correctly?

Is the paragraph well organized, well developed, and clear?

Explaining Effects

Effects are the same as results. Effects can be negative, positive, or both.

A paragraph about effects should include these parts:

A topic sentence: Include the situation (what happened or what you did). Then list the positive or negative results. Use expressions like *several effects, two important results, three major effects*, etc.

Supporting sentences: List each effect and include one or more sentences to explain it. Separate the effects with listing signals such as *The first effect, the second result, next, third,* and *finally*.

A concluding sentence: Summarize the effects and restate or refer back to your topic sentence. Explain how you feel or what may happen in the future.

Use these signal words and phrases to talk about effects.

Signal words: therefore, as a result, consequently

Notes: Use these expressions between two complete sentences. The first sentence states a situation or cause. The second sentence states the effect. Always place a comma after these signal words.

i.e.: The economy is in a recession. Therefore, many people have lost their jobs.

Signal word: so

Notes: Use *so* in compound sentences. Place a comma before it.

i.e.: I don't want to disturb my neighbors, so I always keep my dog indoors at night.

SUGGESTING SOLUTIONS TO A PROBLEM

Presentation

Model Paragraph

Overcoming Insomnia

Many people have trouble falling asleep at night. This problem is called insomnia, and it has many causes. Some people have insomnia because of stress. They lie in bed and think about their problems. Other people have insomnia because of what they eat or drink. Some foods contain chemicals that keep people awake. There are also many people who don't know exactly why they can't fall sleep—they just can't. No matter what the reason, insomnia makes people feel terrible the next day, and too much insomnia can even make a person sick. But luckily there are several ways to solve the problem of insomnia. First, you should have a strict sleep schedule. Go to bed and get up at the same time every day, and don't take naps. This routine can train the body to sleep better at night. Also, in the evening, you had better stay away from food and drinks that have caffeine, like chocolate and coffee. Caffeine keeps people awake. Also, smoking can cause insomnia, so don't smoke at night. Next, try to create a peaceful situation at night. Turn off the TV and the computer one hour before bedtime. Make sure your bedroom is quiet, dark, and cool. Last, if you can't get to sleep, try reading a relaxing book until you start to feel sleepy. These solutions have helped many people who have trouble falling asleep. If you have insomnia, try them and see if they help you, too.

Write a paragraph about one of the topics listed below (or the topic your teacher assigns). You will have 50 minutes.

1 Traffic jams are a problem in all cities. Describe the problem and suggest some solutions.

2 Many people find it difficult to look for a job. Describe the problems and suggest some solutions.

3 Many people try to lose weight, but few are successful. Describe the challenges and suggest some solutions.

Editing Checklist

Are the grammar, sentence structure, mechanics, and punctuation correct?

Is the vocabulary appropriate? Are the words spelled correctly?

Is the paragraph well organized, well developed, and clear?

Suggesting Solutions to a Problem

Some paragraphs state or describe a problem. Then they list solutions to the problem. A problem-solution paragraph should include these parts:

The topic sentence: The topic sentence should name the problem. It can also mention the cause or causes of the problem. For example: *Many people who work on a computer all day have pain in their hands, neck, and back.*

Supporting sentences: Divide the body of your paragraph into two parts. Explain or describe the causes of the problem in the first part. Then explain and describe the solution or solutions.

You should write a major transition between the problem and the solutions.

For example: *If you are suffering from hand or back pain because of computer use, there are several things you can do to solve the problem.*

The concluding sentence: Say or predict how the solutions you listed will solve the problem. If possible, end with a sentence stating that the situation will improve in the future.

Special Writing Skills

WRITING A JOURNAL ENTRY

Model Paragraph

Karen Taylor

July 17, 2012

Topic: Write about your first day in a new country.

Last year, I went to Poland for three months to study Polish and teach English. It was the first time I traveled abroad. I remember how I felt when the airplane landed. I looked around and everyone was speaking Polish. I didn't speak any Polish except for some small easy phrases, so I felt completely lost. Also, all the signs were in Polish. I didn't see or hear any English anywhere! I was scared. I wondered if I had made the right decision. I walked to the baggage area and saw a middle-aged, smiling woman holding up a sign with my name on it. I guessed she was my host mother. As soon as she saw me, she gave me a huge hug! I felt surprised but much more comfortable after that. We collected my bags and walked to her car. She talked to me the whole way, in Polish. I couldn't understand her, but I liked how she made me feel. As she drove me to her house, she showed me the local sights. I began to feel excited about my three months abroad. My host mother really helped me feel comfortable on my first day in Poland.

Write a journal entry about one of the topics listed below or about the topic your teacher assigns. You will have 50 minutes.

1 Write about what you did today or yesterday.

2 Write about something you learned today.

Editing Checklist

Are the grammar, sentence structure, mechanics, and punctuation correct?

Is the vocabulary appropriate? Are the words spelled correctly?

Is the paragraph well organized, well developed, and clear?

Writing a Journal Entry

Journal writing is a kind of personal writing. There are different kinds of journals. For example, there are private diaries that only the writer sees. There are also topic journals, in which a teacher may ask you to respond to a question or write about a topic that he or she provides. Topic journals are also called "guided response journals."

Here are general guidelines for journal writing.

If you're writing a diary, keep a special notebook or place on your computer just for writing in your journal. Many people enjoy writing their journals by hand with a special pen.

Write the date and perhaps your location at the beginning of every journal entry.

If you're writing a diary, be creative. For example, try writing in different places, or illustrate your journal entries with drawings.

If you're writing a diary, don't worry too much about spelling, punctuation, or vocabulary. Journal writing is personal. The point is to allow your thoughts and feelings to flow from your mind to the paper.

If you are writing a topic journal, write your name, the date, and the topic or question at the top of your paper.

WRITING AN EMAIL

Presentation

Model Informal Email

From: Marcie.thomas@gmail.com

Date: October 18, 2011 10:35:50 AM PST

To: Kendra.smith@yahoo.com

Subject: Get together about sociology project?

Hey Kendra!

What are you doing later today? Want to get together maybe after dinner to work on our sociology project? I have a lot of ideas, but I need to get your opinion. Also, did you write down the homework from yesterday's class? I wasn't there, so I need to get that ASAP. If you have it, LMK! Call me about getting together after dinner, ok? Thx!

Talk soon,

Marcie

Write an email about one of the topics listed below or about the topic your teacher assigns. You will have 50 minutes.

1 Write an email to a friend inviting him or her to get together.

2 Write an email to a teacher asking for information about your class or an assignment.

Editing Checklist

Are the grammar, sentence structure, mechanics, and punctuation correct?

Is the vocabulary appropriate? Are the words spelled correctly?

Is the email well organized, well developed, and clear?

Writing an Email

There are two kinds of emails: personal and business. Personal emails are like personal letters. They use informal language and abbreviations. Business emails are like business letters. The language is formal.

Here are general guidelines for writing an email.

Write the topic of your email in the subject line. This is especially important in a business email.

Use appropriate openings and closings. For personal emails these can be quite casual. For business emails you should be more formal.

In a personal email you don't need to worry too much about spelling, punctuation, or vocabulary. You can use contractions, incomplete sentences, abbreviations like LMK (Let Me Know) or "Thx" (Thanks), emoticons like ☺, exclamation points, and capital letters to indicate strong feelings.

In contrast, a business email should be written well. Write complete sentences and avoid casual abbreviations. Be polite and professional. You should proofread to make sure there are no mistakes.

_____

_____

_____

_____

_____

_____

_____

_____

_____

_____

_____

_____

_____

_____

_____

_____

_____

WRITING A SUMMARY

Model Summary

Summary of *The Alchemist*

The book *The Alchemist* by Paolo Coelho is about following your dream. In the story, a poor boy named Santiago has a repeating dream about a treasure waiting for him at the pyramids in Egypt. He lives in Spain, but he decides to travel to Egypt to see if his dream is true. First, he goes to Morocco. He has many troubles there, but finally he joins a group of people traveling across the desert. During the trip, they stop at an oasis, where Santiago meets two very important people. First, he falls in love with a woman named Fatima. Second, he meets a very wise man who is an alchemist. This means he can turn metal into gold. Even though Santiago now wants to stay in the oasis, the alchemist and Fatima both convince him to continue following his dream. The alchemist travels with the boy to Egypt. During the trip, they have many difficult situations, and the boy learns a lot of important lessons. Eventually, they get to the pyramids, and the alchemist leaves Santiago to find his treasure by himself. While Santiago is digging, something happens that makes him understand that the treasure he is looking for is actually back in Spain. He returns to Spain and finds the treasure—an old box of very rare jewels and gold—right under the place where he lived. However, the treasure means much more now because his journey changed him into a better person.

Write a summary about one of the topics listed below or about the topic your teacher assigns. You will have 50 minutes.

1. Write a summary of a movie you are familiar with. Describe who was in it and what happened.
2. Write a summary of some news you heard about recently. Describe who or what it was about and what happened.

Editing Checklist

Are the grammar, sentence structure, mechanics, and punctuation correct?

Is the vocabulary appropriate? Are the words spelled correctly?

Is the summary well organized, well developed, and clear?

Writing a Summary

A summary is a concise piece of writing written in your own words that gives the main ideas of a longer work, such as a book, a movie, or a magazine article. It should express a sense of the larger work, while also pointing to aspects that you feel are especially important. A summary should be organized the same way as paragraphs.

A good summary includes these parts:

Topic sentence: Include the name of the piece you are summarizing, the author (or director, or musician), and the topic.

Body: Include the main ideas from the work. A good way to organize the main ideas is to ask the questions who, what, when, where, why, and how.

Conclusion: You can include the author's conclusions or write your own. For example, you can write the answers to these questions: Did the work help you or change you in some way? Will you remember the work? Why? Will you recommend it to other people? Why or why not?

_____
_____
_____
_____
_____
_____
_____
_____
_____
_____
_____
_____
_____
_____
_____
_____
_____
_____

WRITING A PERSONAL LETTER

Model Personal Letter

143 Front Street
Philadelphia, PA 19133

May 10, 2012

Dear Mom and Dad,

How is everything? I hope you both are doing well. I'm sorry I haven't called in a few days, but things have been crazy over here. I have final exams in two weeks, and I have been studying a lot. I'm really scared about my physics exam. At least my literature exam will be easy. I have to write an essay on *Hamlet*, but writing isn't that hard for me, as you know.

Do you remember my friends Megan and Zoe? You met them at the barbeque during Parents' Weekend. Anyway, we were thinking about going to the beach for a few days after exams are over. We want to rent a beach house with a few other friends. It will be really fun, and after all our hard work this semester we really need a break!

Renting a beach house is expensive though, and I don't have a lot of extra money. I spent a lot on textbooks and food this semester. So, can I borrow some money for this trip? I promise I'll be able to pay you back after my summer job starts. Please let me know.

Love you both!

Norah

Write a personal letter about one of the topics listed below or about the topic your teacher assigns. You will have 50 minutes.

1 Write a personal letter to a friend telling him or her about what you did this week.

2 Write a personal letter to a family member telling him or her about your plans for next week.

Editing Checklist

Are the grammar, sentence structure, mechanics, and punctuation correct?

Is the vocabulary appropriate? Are the words spelled correctly?

Is the letter well organized, well developed, and clear?

Writing a Personal Letter

These days most people use email or other electronic devices to keep in touch, but many people still enjoy writing and receiving personal letters. Personal letters are also called "friendly letters." You write them to a friend or relative.

Personal letters normally include information about your life. They are informal and are often handwritten.

Personal letters typically include these parts:

Date

Greeting

Body / Message

Closing

Signature

Keep these tips in mind when you write a personal letter:

The greeting and closing are followed by commas (for example: Dear Bob,; Love, Adam)

Use informal language. In other words, write the way you speak.

Remember to ask questions and show interest in the person you are writing to.

_____

_____

_____

_____

_____

_____

_____

_____

_____

WRITING A BUSINESS LETTER

Presentation

Model Business Letter

12502 Burbank Boulevard
Los Angeles, CA 91404

July 10, 2012

Fitness For You Corporate Office
13496 Denton Boulevard
Los Angeles, CA 92854

To Whom It May Concern:

I am writing to cancel my membership at your gym. I have been a member of this gym for five years, but lately I have noticed that the quality has suffered. When I first joined, your gym was clean, modern, and friendly, but that has changed. A lot of the equipment is broken all the time, and the locker rooms are a mess. I even saw three cockroaches in the showers the last time I was there. Also, the people who work at the front desk are rude. They just look at their phones the whole time. They don't talk to anyone, and it makes me feel insignificant.

I have complained about these problems, but nobody did anything to address them. And now I notice that you are raising your prices. This is wrong, and I cannot agree to be a member of your gym anymore.

Please cancel my membership immediately.

Thank you in advance.

Sincerely,

Alexandra Smith
Alexandra Smith

Write a business letter about one of the topics listed below or about the topic your teacher assigns. You will have 50 minutes.

1 Write a letter to the manager of a restaurant or store. Tell the manager about the great service you received at his or her business.

2 Write a letter to the manager of a hotel. Complain to the manager about the terrible service you received at that hotel.

Editing Checklist

Are the grammar, sentence structure, mechanics, and punctuation correct?

Is the vocabulary appropriate? Are the words spelled correctly?

Is the letter well organized, well developed, and clear?

Writing a Business Letter

Business letters are more formal than personal letters or emails. You usually write business letters to people you don't know. For example, you can write a business letter to ask for information, to thank someone for something, to complain, or to respond to a letter the sender sent you.

These days most business letters have a "block" format. This means all the writing starts on the left side and the first lines of the paragraphs are not indented. Business letters typically have the following six parts:

Heading. The heading includes your address and the date, but not your name. It is written in the upper left-hand corner of the paper.

Inside address. This is the name, title, company name, and address of the person you are writing to.

Greeting. Write a formal greeting and put a colon after it. For example:

Dear Sir or Madam:

To Whom It May Concern:

Dear Dr. Swenson:

Body. This is your main message. Identify yourself and say the reason for your letter at the beginning. Then give additional details. At the end of this part, say what action, if any, you want the person or institution to take. Thank the person to whom you are writing if it is appropriate.

Closing. Use a formal closing and put a comma after it. For example:

Sincerely,

Yours truly,

Best wishes,

Signature. Handwrite your signature. Then type your name under it.

Here are additional tips for writing business letters:

- Use formal language. Do not use slang. Do not try to be funny.
- Do not ask personal questions or discuss your personal life.
- Type. Do not handwrite a business letter.

APPENDICES

Appendix 1
Common Irregular Verbs

Base Form	Simple Past	Base Form	Simple Past
be	was, were	keep	kept
become	became	know	knew
begin	began	leave	left
bite	bit	lose	lost
blow	blew	make	made
break	broke	meet	met
bring	brought	pay	paid
build	built	put	put
buy	bought	read	read
catch	caught	run	ran
choose	chose	say	said
come	came	see	saw
cost	cost	sell	sold
cut	cut	send	sent
do	did	sing	sang
drink	drank	sit	sat
drive	drove	sleep	slept
eat	ate	speak	spoke
fall	fell	spend	spent
feel	felt	stand	stood
find	found	steal	stole
fly	flew	swim	swam
forget	forgot	take	took
get	got	teach	taught
give	gave	tell	told
go	went	think	thought
grow	grew	throw	threw
have	had	understand	understood
hear	heard	wake up	woke up
hold	held	wear	wore
hurt	hurt	write	wrote

Appendix 2

Transitions Overview

Transition signals are words or phrases that connect ideas. These signals connect your sentences to make your writing more coherent.

To give examples	To indicate time order	To indicate order of importance
for example for instance such as	at 8:00 a.m. at the time after (a while) after that before lunch finally first, second, third, etc. first of all in 1987 in the morning / afternoon / evening later next now on March 4 soon then to begin	also another (example, characteristic) first, second, third, etc. first of all finally in addition most importantly most of all next one (way, reason, etc.) the most important (reason, point, advantage, etc.) is . . . the next / second / last (point, problem, etc.) is (that)

Appendix 3

Confusing Words

These are words that students sometimes confuse. They sound similar, but they have different meanings. You can always check the meanings of words in your dictionary.

1 Accept / Except

Accept is a verb. It means "to receive something offered with gladness."

He **accepted** the job.

Except is a preposition. It is used to show things or people that are not included in a statement. It means "other than."

Everybody came to the party **except** Ellen.

2 Advice / Advise

Advice is a noun. It means "a suggestion about what should be done about a situation."

My brother gave me good **advice.**

Advise is a verb. It means "to tell someone what you think he or she should do." When you **advise**, you offer **advice.**

I'm confused. What do you **advise** me to do?

3 Affect / Effect

Affect is a verb. It means "to have an influence on."

The medicine **affected** her badly.

Effect is a noun. It is a result produced by a cause.

The medicine did not have any **effect** on her.

Effect is also a verb. It means "to result in."

Technology **effected** change in the way people communicate.

4 Sight / Site

Sight is a noun. It means "the ability to see."

He lost his **sight** in a car accident, and now he is blind.

Site is also a noun. It is a place or location of something.

There are several possible **sites** for the new museum.

5 Every day / Everyday

Every day is an adverbial phrase. It means "each day."

I brush my teeth twice **every day**.

Everyday is an adjective. It means usual or ordinary.

For most people, stress is a part of **everyday** life.

6 For / Four

For is a preposition. It has many meanings. For example, it indicates the purpose of something.

This machine is **for** blending fruit.

Four is a number.

I have **four** sisters.

7 Its / It's

Its is a possessive adjective. It means "belonging to something."

The tree lost all **its** leaves.

It's is a contraction. It means "it is."

It's a nice day. Let's go to the beach.

8 Loose / Lose

Loose is an adjective. It refers to something that is movable or not fixed.

I lost weight, so these pants are **loose** on me.

Lose is a verb. It means "to come to be without."

I **lost** my cell phone.

Lose can also mean "to fail to win."

We **lost** a game.

9 Right / Write

Right is an adjective. It means "correct."

Your answer is **right**.

Write is a verb. It means "to produce symbols on a surface."

I need to **write** a paper for my history class.

10 Their / There / They're

Their is a possessive adjective. It means "belonging to them."

Where is **their** house?

There is an adverb. It means "in or near a particular location."

Please put the books **there**.

They're is a contraction. It means "they are."

They're too tired to go to the party.

11 To / Too / Two

To is a preposition. It has many meanings. For example, it means "in the direction of."

We drove **to** the store.

Too is an adverb. It means "also."

Joe has blond hair, and his sister does, **too**.

Two is a number.

The family owns **two** cars.

12 Weather / Whether

Weather is a noun. It refers to the state of the atmosphere at a certain time and place.

In good **weather**, Jane likes to walk to work.

Whether is a conjunction. It means "if."

I don't know **whether** I will go to the party (or not).

13 Who's / Whose

Who's is a contraction. It means "who is."

Who's that man talking with our teacher?

Whose is a possessive adjective. It's used to ask which person or thing something belongs to.

Whose phone is this?

14 You're / Your

You're is a contraction. It means "you are."

You're late.

Your is a possessive adjective. It means "something belongs to you."

Is that **your** dog?

Appendix 4
Subordinating Conjunctions

Subordinating conjunctions are words that introduce dependent clauses. The following are common categories of subordinating conjunctions:

To introduce time clauses	
Conjunctions	**Examples**
after	We washed the dishes **after** we finished eating.
as soon as	I'll help you **as soon as** I get off the phone.
before	**Before** you can get a driver's license, you have to take a test.
when	**When** Ella finishes college, she plans to travel.
while	I waited in the car **while** my friend was in the supermarket.
To introduce clauses of reason	
Conjunctions	**Examples**
because	Jack was late to work **because** his car had a flat tire.
since	**Since** he loves high-calorie foods, Bob is overweight.
To introduce conditions	
Conjunction	**Examples**
if	**If** I don't eat breakfast, I get very hungry around 9 a.m.

Appendix 5
Coordinating Conjunctions

The coordinating conjunctions are **and**, **or**, **but**, and **so**. Use them to connect words, phrases, or clauses.

Conjunctions	Examples
and	I like sandwiches with peanut butter **and** jelly.
	Mary washed the dishes, **and** John cleaned the floor.
or	You can go downtown by bus **or** by subway.
	This weekend we'll stay home and paint the garage, **or** we'll go visit my mother in Miami.
but	Eric is very tall **but** very thin.
	Karen has a new smartphone, **but** she doesn't know how to use it.
so	Abby's flight to Chicago was late, **so** she missed her connecting flight to Toronto.

Appendix 6

Subject, Object, and Possessive Pronouns and Possessive Adjectives

Forms	Singular	Plural
Subject pronouns	I, you, he, she, it	we, you, they
Object pronouns	me, you, him, her, it	us, you, them
Possessive pronouns	mine, yours, his, hers, its	ours, yours, theirs
Possessive adjectives	my, your, his, her, its	our, your, their

Appendix 7

Prepositions of Time and Place

Prepositions of time tell us *when* something happens. Prepositions of place tell us *where* something is. Notice that some of the prepositions can be used to talk both about time and place.

Prepositions of Time		Examples
Use *in* with	parts of the day	in the morning, in the evening
	months	in December
	years	in 1975
	seasons	in the summer
Use *on* with	days of the week	on Tuesday
	specific dates	on November 13th
	holidays	on Thanksgiving
	special days	on my birthday
Use *at* with	specific times	at 3 o'clock, at 6 p.m.
Use *from … to* with	a span of time	from 2 to 4 a.m., from Monday to Friday, from January to June

Prepositions of Place	Examples
above	There's a clock **above** the bookcase.
across from	There is a sofa **across from** the desk.
beside, next to	There's a lamp **beside / next to** the computer table
between	There's a sofa **between** the cabinets.
in front of	There's a chair **in front of** the desk.
in the middle of	There's a table **in the middle of** the room.
in, inside	There are clothes **in / inside** the closet.
on	There are lots of papers **on** the desk.
on both sides of	There are potted plants **on both sides of** the sofa.
on the (your) right, on the (your) left	When you enter the room, the closet is **on the right**. There's a bookcase **on the left**.
on top of	There's a computer **on top of** the computer table.
outside	There is a hallway **outside** the office.
over	There are windows **over** the sofa.
under	There are power cords **under** the computer table.

Appendix 8
Common Noncount Nouns

Noncount nouns are nouns that can't be counted. They are always singular.

advice	history	pepper
beauty	homework	pollution
biology	ice	rain
bread	ice cream	rice
broccoli	information	salt
butter	jewelry	sand
cheese	juice	snow
chemistry	lettuce	soup
coffee	love	spaghetti
corn	luck	sugar
crime	mail	tea
fish	math	time
food	meat	traffic
fruit	milk	vocabulary
furniture	money	water
garbage	music	weather
geography	noise	work
happiness	oil	
help	paper	

Appendix 9
Spelling Rules
Spelling of Plural Count Nouns

Rules	Singular	Plural
Add -s to form the plural of most count nouns.	pencil	pencils
	cat	cats
Add -es to form the plural of nouns that end in a consonant + o.	tomato	tomatoes
Add -es to form the plural of nouns that end in *ch, sh, x,* or *ss.*	kiss	kisses
	box	boxes
	witch	witches
	wish	wishes
To form the plural of words that end in consonant + y, change the y to *i* and add -es.	party	parties
To form the plural of words that end in vowel + y, add -s.	boy	boys
Some nouns do not have a singular form.		clothes
		pants
Some plural nouns have an irregular plural form.	child	children
	foot	feet
	man	men
	person	people
	tooth	teeth
	woman	women

Spelling of Third-Person Singular Present Verbs

Rules	Base Form	Third Person
Add -s to form the third-person singular of most present singular verbs.	walk	walks
Add -es to verbs ending in s, z, x, sh, and ch.	kiss	kisses
	buzz	buzzes
	fix	fixes
	push	pushes
	watch	watches
If a verb ends in consonant + y, then change the y to i and add -es.	try	tries
If a verb ends in vowel + y, then do not change the ending.	pay	pays
Have, be, and do have irregular third-person singular forms.	be	is
	do	does
	have	has

Spelling of Present Participles

Rules	Base Form	Present Participle
Add -ing to the base form of most verbs.	walk	walking
If a verb ends in -e, drop the e and add -ing.	come	coming
If a one-syllable verb ends in a consonant + vowel + consonant (CVC), then double the last consonant and add -ing.	sit	sitting
Do not double the last consonant if a word ends in w, x, or y.	flow	flowing
	fix	fixing
	play	playing
In words of more than one syllable that end in consonant + vowel + consonant (CVC), double the last consonant if the syllable is stressed.	permit	permitting

Rules	Base Form	Past Tense
If a verb ends in a consonant, add -ed.	jump	jumped
If a verb ends in -e, add -d.	like	liked
If a verb ends in consonant + y, then change the y to i and add -ed.	carry	carried
If the verb ends in vowel + y, then do not change the y to i. Just add -ed.	play	played
If a one-syllable verb ends in consonant + vowel + consonant (CVC), then double the last consonant and add -ed.	jog	jogged
Do not double the last consonant if a word ends in w, x, or y. Just add -ed.	fix	fixed
	bow	bowed
In words of more than one syllable that end in consonant + vowel + consonant (CVC), double the last consonant and add -ed.	permit	permitted

Appendix 10
Modals

Modal verbs are different from regular verbs:

- They have only one form, without an –s or –ed ending.
- They are followed by the base form of the verb, without to.
- They have different meanings.

You *can* swim (you are able to swim).

You *may* swim (I am allowing you to swim).

Can, Can't, Could, and *Couldn't*

The modals *can, can't,* and *could* are used to talk about

- ability in the present and past
- possibility in the present and future (affirmative only)

Study the forms and meanings of these modals.

Time	Ability	Possibility
Present / Future	John **can** swim.	It **could / can** rain this afternoon.
	Betsy **can't / cannot** cook.	I **can / could** stop by your house later.
	Can Andrew sing?	
Past	When I was a child, I **could** speak Korean.	*(none)*
	I **couldn't** drive a car.	

Should, Ought to, and *Had Better*

The modals *should, ought to,* and *had better* are used to give advice or suggestions in the present / future.

Should and *ought to* are similar in meaning. *Should* is more common.

Had better is more urgent and imperative than *should / ought to.* It means there will be a bad result if the advice is not followed.

Modals	Examples
should, shouldn't (should not), ought to	You **should / ought to** get more exercise.
	You **shouldn't** drink coffee at night.
had better, had better not	We're almost out of gas. **We'd better** stop at a gas station.
	I need to study this evening. **I'd better** not go out.

May or *Might*

The modals *may* and *might* are used to talk about present and future possibilities.

- *May* and *might* are similar in meaning.
- Do not contract the negative forms *may not* and *might not.*

Modals	Examples
may, might	It **might** rain this afternoon.
	I **may** go to a movie now.
may not, might not	George **may not** graduate this semester.
	Hannah **might not** want to go.

Would Rather

Would rather expresses preference in the present or future.

- Affirmative sentences have short forms and long forms with *than.*
- Do not use contractions in questions with *would rather.*

Forms	Examples	Meanings
Affirmatives	I **would rather / I'd rather** walk than drive to the theater.	I prefer to walk.
	I'd rather walk.	
Negatives	I **would rather / I'd rather** not eat here.	I prefer not to eat here.
Yes/No questions	**Would** you **rather** walk or drive to the theater?	Do you prefer to walk or drive?
Wh- questions	What **would** you **rather** have, fish or meat?	Do you want fish or meat?

Appendix 11
Descriptive Adjectives

Categories	Examples
Quantity	two books, many horses, a lot of time
Opinion / Condition	a beautiful woman
Condition	a broken window
Size	a huge wave, a tiny kitten
Shape	a square picture, a round cake
Age	an old dog
Color	a dark night, a blue lake
Origin	an American painter
Material	a wood table
Purpose	a salad plate
Noun used as adjective	coffee cup, wedding dress

Appendix 12
Adverbs of Frequency and Manner

Adverbs of Frequency

Here are some general rules for placing adverbs of frequency in a sentence.

Rules	Examples
Adverbs of frequency usually come before the main verb.	Cora **often** takes the train to work.
	She **sometimes** rides her bike.
	She **never** walks.
Adverbs of frequency usually come after a form of *be*.	Manolo is **never** late.
	Mr. Canning is **seldom** angry.
Some adverbs of frequency—*usually, frequently, often, sometimes, occasionally*—can also come at the beginning or end of the sentence.	**Frequently** the train is late.
	David works at home **sometimes**.

Adverbs of Manner

Adverbs of manner give information about verbs. They tell *how* you do something.

Rules	Examples
Adverbs of manner cannot come between the verb and the object.	<u>Correct</u>: She made the bed **neatly**.
	<u>Incorrect</u>: She made neatly the bed.
Most adjectives of manner end in *-ly*. A few adverbs have the same form as adjectives: *fast, high, low, hard, late, early.*	<u>Correct</u>: Martina jogs **fast**.
	<u>Incorrect</u>: Martina jogs fastly.
Adverbs of manner can come in different places in the sentence. They can come after the verb.	The car stopped **suddenly**.
They can come before the verb.	She **quickly** closed the door.
They can come at the beginning of the sentence (followed by a comma).	**Sadly,** she put the photograph in the box.
They can come at the end of the sentence.	The old man stood up **slowly**.

Post-Test 1

In the timed Post-Test 1, you will demonstrate how well you understand sentence structure, grammar, punctuation, mechanics, and organization. You have 50 minutes to complete the test. Circle the answer of the correct choice.

1 Jennifer is _____ her sister.
   a seriouser
   b more serious than
   c more seriouser
   d serious

2 Peter _____ .
   a hit hardly the table
   b hit the table hardly
   c hit the table hard
   d hit hard the table

3 Jorge _____ with his wife.
   a eats always dinner
   b dinner always eats
   c always eats dinner
   d eats dinner always

4 Before our trip to Paris, we need _____ about renting a car.
   a an information
   b informations
   c the information
   d some information

5 Gerald will move to New York if he _____ a job there.
   a will find
   b finds
   c found
   d is finding

6 Johann _____ three languages.
   a can speak
   b can to speak
   c cans speak
   d can speaking

7 Erin _____ a doctor about her cough.

   a shoulds see

   b should see

   c should to see

   d should sees

8 Kevin _____ basketball than baseball.

   a would rather play

   b rather would play

   c rather would plays

   d woulds rather play

9 They usually take their vacation _____ August.

   a on

   b from

   c at

   d in

10 Please hang your coat _____ the closet.

   a inside

   b under

   c between

   d over

11 My grandfather _____ spicy food.

   a enjoys

   b enjoying

   c enjoy

   d is enjoy

12 The workers _____ a break right now.

   a taking

   b are taking

   c take

   d is taking

13 It _____ every day last week.

   a rain

   b raining

   c rained

   d was rain

14 I'm going to visit my grandparents in Florida next _____ .

   a Summer

   b august

   c christmas

   d June

15 The house was dark and cold _____ .

   a , when I arrived

   b when I arrived

   c when, I arrived

   d when I, arrived

16 Some people love to travel _____ others prefer to stay home.

   a and

   b and,

   c , and

   d , and,

17 Robert baked a cake _____ he made a salad.

   a , next,

   b next

   c , next

   d . Next,

18 Regina is a full-time student _____ she has a part-time job.

   a . In addition,

   b in addition

   c in addition,

   d , in addition,

19 "I have a surprise for you _____ Sergey announced.

   a ."

   b "

   c ,

   d ,"

20 Jim and Katie were married on _____ .

   a September 8, 2005

   b September, 8, 2005

   c September 8 / 2005

   d September 8 2005

21 We went out to dinner _____ a movie.

   a and saw,

   b , and saw

   c and then we saw

   d , and then we saw

22 Gail is a vegetarian, _____ she never eats meat.

   a but

   b so

   c and

   d or

23 Normally, children learn how to talk _____ they can read.

    a before

    b after

    c as soon as

    d while

24 We couldn't sleep _____ it was so hot.

    a because

    b for

    c if

    d then

25 The children ran outside _____ .

    a , as soon as it stopped raining

    b it stopped raining

    c as soon as it stopped raining

    d as soon as, it stopped raining

26 Ahmed thanked the woman _____ helped him.

    a , who

    b , that

    c who

    d which

27 The directions that my sister gave me _____ very clear.

    a is

    b are

    c be

    d was

28 Circle the complete sentence.

    a If Pari decides to go to medical school.

    b Apple juice my son's favorite drink.

    c Green tea has several medical benefits.

    d George W. Bush, the 43rd president of the United States.

29 Circle the incorrect sentence.

    a Lidia loves to swim. She goes to the pool every day.

    b Lidia loves to swim, and she goes to the pool every day.

    c Lidia loves to swim and goes to the pool every day.

    d Lidia loves to swim she goes to the pool everyday.

30 Circle the incorrect sentence.

    a I love my new apartment because it has a lot of light.

    b love my new apartment, it has a lot of light.

    c I love my new apartment. It has a lot of light.

    d Because it has a lot of light, I love my new apartment.

31 Yesterday I spent a fun morning with my cousin Barbara. To start the day, she came to my house, and I made French toast with whipped cream and strawberries. It was delicious! _____ , we took my dog for a walk around the neighbourhood. We saw some neighbors, and I introduced my cousin to them.

a After

b After that

c Late

d Now

32 A good language teacher has several important qualities. First of all, a good teacher has knowledge of the subject. If the subject is English, the teacher should be an expert on English grammar, vocabulary, and pronunciation. Second, a good teacher needs to care about her students. If a student is having a problem, for example, the teacher should spend time talking to the student and trying to help. _____ , a good teacher knows how to explain information clearly. For example, she should use words that her students understand, and she shouldn't speak too fast.

a Another

b Therefore

c Most importantly

d Because

33 The City Art Museum is not well organized. It consists of four rooms. As you enter the museum, you enter a room with 19th century American landscapes by artists such as William Paxton and Edward Hicks. The room _____ the first one contains sculptures from different time periods. Some are very ancient and others are quite modern. Continuing to walk, you come to a room that contains religious paintings from different countries. The last room contains contemporary American paintings. For example, there is a painting by Andy Warhol of a can of soup.

a between

b in the center

c on the end

d behind

34 Millions of Americans suffer from back pain. Many people develop back pain _____ they spend too much time sitting at their desks.

a because of

b result

c because

d therefore

35 Getting a full-time job has had several negative effects on my health. First, I don't have enough time to exercise. _____ , I have gained five pounds since I started this job.

a Because of

b And

c Since

d Therefore

36 My two best friends, Amy and Sandra, are similar in several ways. First, Amy is a lawyer. Her specialty is family law. _____ , Sandra is a lawyer. She works for the U.S. government.

    a Like

    b Similarly

    c Alike

    d Same

37 The *Boeing 737* and *Boeing 747* are very different airplanes. First, the *737* is a narrow-body plane used for flying medium distances. _____ , the *747* is a wide-body plane that can fly long distances.

    a Similarly

    b Different

    c In contrast

    d Then

38 _____ it should be illegal for people to use cell phones in movie theaters. I have several reasons for my opinion.

    a I think that

    b According to me,

    c I am against

    d Because

39 Many things, _____ paper, silk, and noodles, were invented by the ancient Chinese. First of all, paper was invented more than 2,000 years ago.

    a first

    b such as

    c both

    d likewise

40 Which words in the following topic sentence are the controlling idea? (The controlling idea tells what specific details the paragraph will discuss.)

    Topic sentence: The process of writing a research paper for a college class involves four stages.

    a the process

    b writing a research paper

    c a college class

    d involves four stages

Post–Test 2

In the timed Post-Test 2, you will demonstrate how well you can write about a topic. Pay attention to sentence structure, grammar, punctuation, mechanics, organization, and vocabulary.

Write about the following topic or the topic your teacher assigns.

You have 50 minutes to complete the test.

> Write a paragraph telling your life story. When and where were you born? What was your childhood like? Where did you go to school? What are you doing now?

_____

_____

_____

_____

_____

_____

_____

_____

_____

_____

_____

_____

_____

_____

_____

_____

_____

_____

ANSWER KEY

PRE-TEST

Pre-Test 1   pp. 1–6
1. a, 2. b, 3. b, 4. d, 5. c, 6. a, 7. c, 8. a,
9. c, 10. b, 11. c, 12. d, 13. b, 14. d, 15. b,
16. a, 17. a, 18. d, 19. b, 20. b, 21. d,
22. d, 23. a, 24. a, 25. b, 26. b, 27. a,
28. c, 29. a, 30. b, 31. b, 32. b, 33. d,
34. b, 35. d, 36. c, 37. d, 38. a, 39. b,
40. d

Pre-Test 2   p. 7
Answers will vary.

PUNCTUATION AND MECHANICS

Capital Letters

PROPER NOUNS AND PRONOUNS

Practice 1   p. 8
1. The, Friday
2. summer, Thailand
3. Where, post office
4. cousin, Yale University
5. French, Spanish
6. gas station, Pico Boulevard
7. Toronto, Thanksgiving
8. Chemistry
9. Christians, Jews, Muslims
10. Italian, pizza
11. semester, January

Practice 2   p. 9
1. friday
2. traditional, thanksgiving
3. robert, washington, university, his, this, psychology
4. when, yasmine, funland, christmas
5. my, i, middle, east
6. cara, wednesday
7. be, adams, avenue
8. kelly, proprintco, seattle

ACRONYMS AND PERSONAL TITLES

Practice 1   pp. 10–11
1. b
2. b
3. b
4. a
5. a
6. a
7. a
8. b
9. b
10. a
11. b

Practice 2   p. 11
1. VW
2. UM
3. UN
4. UK
5. BA
6. DC
7. ASAP *or* asap
8. ATM
9. PIN
10. HIV
11. PRC

Commas

COMMAS IN COMPLEX SENTENCES WITH DEPENDENT CLAUSES

Practice 1 pp. 12–13

1. b	7. a
2. b	8. a
3. a	9. b
4. a	10. a
5. b	11. b
6. b	

Practice 2 pp. 13–14

1. a	7. c
2. b	8. a
3. c	9. b
4. a	10. b
5. c	11. a
6. b	

COMMAS IN COMPOUND SENTENCES WITH COORDINATING CONJUNCTIONS

Practice 1 pp. 15–16

1. b	7. b
2. a	8. b
3. b	9. b
4. a	10. a
5. a	11. b
6. b	

Practice 2 pp. 16–17

1. c	3. a
2. b	4. c

5. a	9. c
6. b	10. a
7. b	11. a
8. c	

COMMAS FOR ITEMS IN A SERIES

Practice 1 pp. 18–19

1. a	7. b
2. b	8. a
3. a	9. b
4. b	10. a
5. a	11. b
6. b	

Practice 2 pp. 19–20

1. c	7. b
2. b	8. c
3. c	9. b
4. a	10. c
5. b	11. a
6. c	

COMMAS WITH TIME AND ORDER SIGNALS

Practice 1 pp. 21–22

1. Then
2. First,
   Then
   Last,
3. after that
   In 2007,
   now
4. At the beginning,
   after that
   by the end

Practice 2 p. 22

1. First,
2. Second,
3. after that
4. Then
5. Finally,
6. To begin,
7. Then
8. Third,
9. by now,
10. after lunch
11. At 2 P.M.,

COMMAS WITH TRANSITION SIGNALS

Practice 1 p. 24

1. a
2. b
3. b
4. b
5. a
6. a
7. a
8. b
9. a
10. a
11. b

Practice 2 pp. 25–26

1. a, b
2. a, c
3. a, c
4. b, c
5. b, c
6. a, b, c, d
7. a
8. a, b
9. a

COMMAS WITH ADJECTIVE CLAUSES

Practice 1 pp. 27–28

1. b
2. b
3. b
4. a
5. b
6. b
7. b
8. b
9. b
10. a
11. a

Practice 2 pp. 28–29

1. the Fourth of July,
2. Belinda, who was tired after studying all night,
3. Tehran, which is the capital of Iran,
4. Madagascar, which is an island in the Indian Ocean,
5. Dr. Afar, who is my dentist
6. Great Danes, which are large dogs,
7. Lufthansa, which is a German airline
8. my health club, which is open 24 hours
9. baklava, which is a rich Middle Eastern cake filled with nuts and honey
10. Jay's house, which has a large living room
11. *The King's Speech*, which won an Oscar,

Letters

PUNCTUATION IN LETTERS

Practice 1 p. 31

1. b
2. a
3. b
4. a
5. b
6. b
7. a
8. b
9. a
10. b
11. b

Practice 2 p. 32

1. b
2. b
3. b
4. a
5. a
6. b
7. a
8. b
9. a
10. b
11. a

The Sentence

SENTENCE PUNCTUATION

Practice 1 pp. 33–34

1. c	7. c
2. b	8. c
3. c	9. b
4. a	10. c
5. a	11. a
6. a	

Practice 2 pp. 34–35

1. Last Saturday was my thirtieth birthday.
2. My husband wanted to take me out to dinner.
3. He asked me to choose a restaurant.
4. I thought about it for a while.
5. What kind of food did I feel like eating?
6. Finally, I chose a French restaurant.
7. He made a reservation for seven o'clock.
8. He made some other plans as well.
9. When we arrived at the restaurant, the host took us to a private room.
10. We walked in, and I saw about ten of our friends sitting there.
11. It was a huge surprise!

Quotations

Practice 1 pp. 36–37

1. b	7. a
2. c	8. c
3. b	9. b
4. b	10. a
5. c	11. c
6. b	

Practice 2 p. 38

1. The president told the nation, "The economy is growing stronger."
2. A little boy told his mother, "Did you know dogs can talk?"
3. "Really? What do they say?" his mother replied.
4. The boy said, "It depends. Big dogs say 'woof-woof'. Little dogs say 'arf arf'."
5. "Spanish dogs have their own language," the mother said. "They say 'guau guau'."
6. "That's funny," the boy said.
7. The mother added, "That's not all. Japanese dogs say 'wan wan,' and Israeli dogs say 'hav hav.'"
8. The boy said, "That's crazy that those dogs speak more languages than I do."

Paragraph Format

Practice 1 p. 40

1. Heading
2. Title
3. Indent
4. Straight left margin
5. Uneven right margin
6. Run-in sentences
7. Final punctuation

Practice 2 p. 41

1. b	6. a
2. a	7. b
3. a	8. a
4. b	9. b
5. b	

GRAMMAR

Adjectives

ADJECTIVES WITH LINKING VERBS

Practice 1 pp. 42–43

1. Correct
2. Incorrect
3. Incorrect
4. Correct
5. Incorrect
6. Correct
7. Incorrect
8. Incorrect
9. Incorrect
10. Incorrect
11. Correct

Practice 2 p. 43

1. The melon tastes sweet.
2. Cathy's joke was funny.
3. The children sound happy.
4. My cat is lazy.
5. Our teacher seems tired.
6. The weather is terrible.
7. The grass feels soft.
8. This watch is old.
9. That job looks easy.
10. The air smells bad.
11. The milk doesn't smell fresh.

ADJECTIVE ORDER AND FORM

Practice 1 p. 44

old
porcelain
coffee
ordinary
special
twenty
white
faded
birthday
little

right
comfortable
small
bad
happy

Practice 2 p. 45

1. small round
2. traditional Greek church
3. gorgeous white silk
4. long lace
5. large Greek
6. formal gray silk
7. huge loud
8. a lot of delicious Greek
9. tiny old Greek
10. many wonderful wedding
11. tall antique silver

COMPOUND ADJECTIVES, NOUN ADJECTIVES, PROPER ADJECTIVES

Practice 1 pp. 46–47

1. a, 2. a, 3. c, 4. b, 5. a, 6. b, 7. c, 8. b, 9. b, 10. c, 11. b

Practice 2 pp. 48–49

1. b, 2. b, 3. b, 4. a, 5. b, 6. c, 7. a, 8. b, 9. b, 10. a, 11. b

COMPARATIVE ADJECTIVES

Practice 1 p. 50

taller
more muscular
darker
curlier
funnier
more easygoing

more talkative

more creative

more organized

better

Practice 2 p. 50

1. more expensive than

2. easier than

3. more dangerous than

4. more expensive than

5. taller than

6. more exciting than

7. better than

8. worse than

9. shorter than

10. messier than

11. more intelligent than

SUPERLATIVE ADJECTIVES

Practice 1 pp. 51–52

1. c, 2. c, 3. c, 4. b, 5. c, 6. b, 7. a, 8. c, 9. b, 10. c, 11. c

Practice 2 p. 53

1. the cleanest

2. the tallest

3. the saltiest

4. the fastest

5. The most popular

6. the most populated

7. the most expensive

8. The worst

9. the most amazing

10. the best

11. the busiest

Adverbs

ADVERBS OF MANNER

Practice 1 p. 55

1. loudly

2. fast

3. beautifully

4. clearly

5. suddenly

6. politely

7. slowly

8. hard

9. quietly

10. sadly

11. Impatiently

Practice 2 p. 55

1. successfully

2. seriously; quickly

3. badly

4. silently

5. fast; slowly

6. well

7. heavily

8. late

ADVERBS OF FREQUENCY

Practice 1 pp. 56–57

1. b, 2. c, 3. a, 4. a, 5. c, 6. a, 7. b, 8. c, 9. c, 10. b, 11. c

Practice 2 pp. 57–58

1. Georgia is never late to work

2. my family always ate dinner together

3. Usually, my father came home

4. many families rarely eat dinner together

5. I am never home

6. My wife often has to work late, too

7. My kids usually have

8. Frequently they get together

9. we always have dinner

10. we sometimes have a family breakfast

11. We often go out to brunch

Future

FUTURE WITH BE GOING TO AND WILL

Practice 1 pp. 60–61

1. c	7. c
2. a	8. a
3. c	9. b
4. b	10. c
5. c	11. c
6. b	

Practice 2 pp. 61–62

1. will graduate

   are going to come / will come

   will be / is going to be

   isn't going to come / will not come

   will take / are going to take

2. I will lend

   'm going to stay

3. 'm not going to be / will not be

   'll wait / 'm going to wait

   won't help / am not going to

   won't ask

FUTURE REAL CONDITIONAL

Practice 1 pp. 63–64

1. have; will meet
2. is; will go
3. doesn't feel; will go
4. will get; drink
5. won't graduate; doesn't pass
6. don't have; will go
7. breaks down; am going to buy

8. will die; don't water
9. will apply; doesn't find
10. are; won't wait
11. won't buy; don't fit

Practice 2 p. 64

1. see; 'll give
2. don't like; 'll take
3. 'll wake up; make
4. don't agree; 'll think
5. 'll come; 're
6. finish; 'll take
7. will repeat; don't understand
8. don't do; won't have
9. take; won't be
10. don't mail; won't arrive
11. won't go; rains

Imperatives

Practice 1 p. 65

place	stop
Look	Remove
set	open
press	pour
Don't leave	enjoy

Practice 2 p. 66

don't use	find
stay	keep
don't turn on	don't go

stop

park

don't touch

remain

Modals

CAN, CAN'T, COULD, AND COULDN'T

Practice 1 pp. 67–68

1. can, could
2. can
3. can't
4. couldn't
5. could
6. can
7. can't
8. couldn't
9. can
10. couldn't
11. Can

    can't

Practice 2 pp. 68–69

1. Alberto can speak English very well
2. and I can't/cannot concentrate
3. you can meet my sister
4. I couldn't/could not open the door
5. Could you use a computer
6. he couldn't/could not remember
7. he could not/couldn't
8. it could rain
9. I can't/cannot leave the house
10. he could run a mile
11. I can never replace it

SHOULD, OUGHT TO, AND HAD BETTER

Practice 1 pp. 70–71

1. b, 2. a, 3. a, 4. b, 5. c, 6. a, 7. b, 8. b, 9. b, 10. a, 11. b

Practice 2 p. 72

1. I should clean it
2. you should come to class
3. You'd better not cross
4. We shouldn't waste water
5. We'd better not park here
6. you ought to visit
7. You shouldn't go there
8. You shouldn't wait for me
9. you'd better take
10. you'd better buy
11. He'd better not forget

MAY AND MIGHT

Practice 1 pp. 73–74

1. b, 2. a, 3. b, 4. b, 5. b, 6. a, 7. b, 8. b, 9. b, 10. b, 11. b

Practice 2 pp. 74–75

1. may go/might go
2. may go/might go
3. may get/might get
4. may not go/might not go
5. may not use/might not use
6. may have/might have
7. may not exist/might not exist
8. may need/might need
9. may not remember/might not remember
10. may drive/might drive
11. may need/might need

WOULD RATHER

Practice 1 pp. 76–78

1. c; f
2. a
3. c
4. c
5. a; e
6. a
7. b
8. a; d
9. b
10. a
11. c

Practice 2 p. 78

1. would rather play; sing
2. would rather walk; drive
3. Would you rather study; go
4. 'd rather take
5. A: would you rather buy
   B: 'd rather buy
6. would rather make; eat
7. would rather work; sit
8. 'd rather get
9. 'd rather stay
10. would rather send; phone
11. 'd rather not sit

Nouns

COUNT AND NONCOUNT NOUNS

Practice 1 pp. 79–80

1. chicken; supermarket
2. plants; animals
3. people
4. students
5. shirts; hat
6. suitcases
7. song
8. roses; garden; week
9. poodle; dog

Practice 2 p. 80

1. some milk
2. Gas
3. money
4. chocolate
5. water
6. some mail
7. privacy
8. rheumatism
9. some help
10. furniture
11. homework

ARTICLES A, AN, AND THE

Practice 1 p. 82

1. a
2. a; The; an; X; X; a; a
3. a; the; a; an
4. the; the; The; a; the; X; X; X; X; a; a

Practice 2 p. 82

1. a; the
2. A; a; the
3. a
4. the
5. The; the
6. a; the
7. The; the
8. a/the; a; the
9. the

Prepositions

PREPOSITIONS OF TIME

Practice 1 pp. 83–84

1. at
2. from; to; in
3. from; to; In
4. on; on; on
5. at; in

Practice 2 p. 84

1. at; on
2. in
3. On
4. at
5. from; to
6. on
7. In
8. in
9. at
10. from; to
11. on; in

PREPOSITIONS OF PLACE

Practice 1 pp. 86–87

1. a
2. b
3. b
4. c
5. b
6. a
7. a
8. b
9. c
10. a
11. a

Practice 2 pp. 87–88

1. b
2. b
3. c
4. b
5. a
6. a
7. c
8. a

PREPOSITIONAL PHRASES

Practice 1 pp. 89–90

1. a, 2. c, 3. b, 4. a, 5. b, 6. a, 7. a, 8. b, 9. c, 10. a, 11. c

Practice 2 p. 91

1. to the corner
2. to the door; with curly hair and a loud bark
3. in my grandparents' house; at the street; of the house; in her garden
4. in the gray suit
5. under the sofa; on the floor; after dinner
6. from my friend; with me; to the beach

Present

THE SIMPLE PRESENT

Practice 1 pp. 93–94

1. c, 2. b, 3. a, 4. b, 5. b, 6. c, 7. b, 8. a, 9. b, 10. a, 11. c

Practice 2 p. 95

1. do not like/don't like
2. has
3. do not need/don't need
4. are; are not/aren't
5. do not want/don't want; prefer
6. have; does not bark/doesn't bark
7. eats; plays
8. is; does not eat/doesn't eat
9. live; do not have/don't have
10. speaks; is not/isn't
11. does not have/doesn't have

THE PRESENT PROGRESSIVE

Practice 1 p. 97

1. want
2. don't need
3. is walking

4. don't hear

5. don't believe

6. are standing

7. look; love

8. are having

9. A: seem
   B: 'm thinking

10. A: are you looking
    B: think
    A: don't see

11. is not having; 's sleeping

Practice 2 p. 97

1. 's washing

2. 're doing

3. 's sleeping

4. aren't running

5. 're not feeling

6. 'm taking

7. is not working

8. A: are seeing
   B: think

9. 're not using

Past

THE SIMPLE PAST

Practice 1 pp. 98–99

1. walked

2. decided

3. didn't hurry

4. stayed

5. continued

6. arrived

7. didn't have; sat

8. watched

9. enjoyed

10. left

11. didn't want; called

Practice 2 p. 99

1. walked

2. were

   caused

   left

   reported

   happened

   warned

   heard

   didn't believe

   didn't leave

   was

   arrived

   killed

   injured

3. celebrated

   went

   visited

   stay

   met

   tried

   wanted

   didn't have

THE PAST PROGRESSIVE

Practice 1 pp. 100–101

1. b	7. b
2. c	8. a
3. b	9. b; e
4. b	10. b
5. c	11. b
6. b	

Practice 2 p. 102

1. was working
2. was walking

   were sleeping

   wasn't snowing

   was standing

   was waiting
3. was listening

   were reading

   was talking

   was eating

   weren't doing

SENTENCE STRUCTURE

Simple Sentences

SUBJECT/VERB COMBINATIONS

Practice 1 pp. 103–104

1. c, 2. a, 3. c, 4. d, 5. b, 6. c, 7. a, 8. d, 9. b, 10. b, 11. d

Practice 2 pp. 104–105

1. Subject: cousins and I

   Verb: went
2. Subject: fox

   Verbs: jumped and disappeared
3. Subject: Dave

   Verbs: awoke and took
4. Subject: Silvio

   Verbs: is and speaks
5. Subject: Sam and Roger

   Verb: had
6. Subject: wife and I

   Verb: are
7. Subject: Mary

   Verb: forgot
8. Subject: Fernanda and Carlos

   Verb: are
9. Subject: Aziz

   Verb: bought
10. Subject: brother and sister

    Verbs: graduated and moved
11. Subject: wedding

    Verbs: started and ended

CONJUNCTIONS AND AND OR

Practice 1 pp. 106–107

1. I.M. Pei and Antoni Gaudi are famous architects.
2. I like strawberries and bananas.
3. Ellen and Jake will take the bus to the party.
4. I can't speak German or Russian.
5. Susan and David will graduate in 2018.
6. Do you own a car or a motorcycle?
7. New York City and Los Angeles have a lot of people.
8. Tom Cruise or Daniel Craig will get the star role in the new action film.

   Tom Cruise and Daniel Craig will get the star roles in the new action film.
9. Would you like chocolate cake or apple pie for dessert?
10. Please give me the hammer and the nails.
11. The country doesn't have mountains or lakes.

Practice 2 pp. 107–108

1. or	7. and
2. or	8. or
3. and	9. and
4. or	10. or
5. or	11. or
6. and	

Compound Sentences
COORDINATING CONJUNCTIONS AND, BUT, OR, AND SO

Practice 1 pp. 109–110

1. b, 2. b, 3. a, 4. b, 5. a, 6. c, 7. c, 8. b, 9. c, 10. b, 11. a

Practice 2 p. 110

1. It's raining, so we can't go to the park.

2. John goes to college, and he likes it.

3. I would love to take a Chinese class, but I don't have time.

   I'd love to take a Chinese class, but I don't have time.

4. Juan might order a steak, or he might get the fish.

5. My mother did not answer the phone, so I left her a message.

   My mother didn't answer the phone, so I left her a message.

6. My boss is an excellent manager, and she is a good listener.

   My boss is an excellent manager, and she's a good listener.

7. I wanted to sing the song, but I couldn't remember the words.

8. The tree is dead, so we have to cut it down.

9. Do you need to leave, or can you stay for dinner?

10. I can send you an email, or I can call you.

11. John lost his textbook, so he could not study for the test. John lost his textbook, so he couldn't study for the test.

NEITHER AND NOT EITHER TO EXPRESS SIMILAR IDEAS

Practice 1 p. 112

1. b, 2. b, 3. b, 4. a, 5. a, 6. b, 7. a, 8. b, 9. b, 10. b, 11. a

Practice 2 p. 113

1. the clothes dryer doesn't either

2. Joan can't either

3. neither do the Smiths

4. neither did his wife

5. bus drivers won't either

6. neither does New Zealand

7. the potatoes didn't either

8. neither was my uncle

9. Steven didn't either

10. the movie wasn't either

SO AND TOO TO EXPRESS SIMILAR IDEAS

Practice 1 p. 115

1. b	7. a
2. b	8. b
3. a	9. b
4. b	10. b
5. b	11. a
6. a	

Practice 2 p. 116

1. so does Japan

2. and my grandparents do too

3. and "Gala" is too

4. and so is Michiko

5. and Oliver does too

6. and so does Spanish food

7. and so are whales

8. and Sheila will too

9. and Cheryl does too

10. and so is Chicago

Complex Sentences

INDEPENDENT AND DEPENDENT CLAUSES

Practice 1 pp. 117–118

1. a, 2. b, 3. b, 4. b, 5. a, 6. a, 7. a, 8. a, 9. b, 10. a, 11. a, 12. a

Practice 2 p. 119

After the guests went home

after all the guests arrive

While we're eating

After we are done

because I forgot my guitar there

As soon as we arrive

if you tell me the name of a bakery

if you want to find a parking place

SUBORDINATING CONJUNCTIONS OF TEMPORALITY

Practice 1 p. 121

after she gets up in the morning

While she's waiting

When the doors open

Before she enters the pool

As soon as she enters the water

While she swims

when she gets out of the pool

before she leaves the pool

When she arrives at the office

Practice 2 p. 121

Paragraph 1

after	while
as soon as	when
before	

Paragraph 2

When	After
While	when
When	As soon as

REASON, CONDITION, AND TIME SUBORDINATORS

Practice 1 pp. 123–124

1. a, 2. a, 3. b, 4. b, 5. a, 6. c, 7. b, 8. b, 9. b, 10. c, 11. a

Practice 2 p. 124

1. because/since	7. since
2. because/since	8. because/since
3. If	9. if
4. because/since	10. Since
5. since/because	11. because/since
6. because/since	

ADJECTIVE CLAUSES

Practice 1 p. 126

1. who	7. that
2. who, that	8. which
3. that	9. who
4. which	10. that
5. who, that	11. which
6. who	

Practice 2 pp. 126–127

1. a, 2. a, 3. b, 4. a, 5. b, 6. a, 7. a, 8. a, 9. a, 10. b, 11. a

The Complete Sentence
SUBJECT AND VERB
Practice 1 pp. 129–130

1. c, 2. c, 3. a, 4. b, 5. a, 6. a, 7. b, 8. a, 9. a, 10. a, 11. a

Practice 2 pp. 130–131

1. b, 2. c, 3. c, 4. b, 5. a, 6. a, 7. b, 8. c, 9. c, 10. c, 11. c

SUBJECT-VERB AGREEMENT
Practice 1 pp. 132–133

1. a, 2. b, 3. a, 4. a, 5. b, 6. a, c, 7. a, 8. a, 9. b, 10. a, 11. a

Practice 2 p. 134

1. have
2. is
3. contain
4. drink
5. has
6. have
7. drink
8. has
9. helps
10. reduces
11. get

SUBJECT, VERB, OBJECT
Practice 1 pp. 135–136

1. money
2. tickets
3. opinions
4. words
5. house, noise
6. keys
7. color, it
8. project
9. man
10. songs
11. movies

Practice 2 p. 136

1. I lost my keys.
2. Indira plays the piano.
3. Mark didn't finish his homework.
4. We need a new car.
5. I don't have any free time.
6. Zara loves bread and butter.
7. Can you bring me a glass of water?
8. All the students passed.
9. Minnesota has more than 10,000 lakes.
10. Tom left an hour ago.
11. Robert Frost wrote many poems about America.

FRAGMENTS
Practice 1 pp. 138–139

1. b, 2. c, 3. a, 4. d, 5. b, 6. c, 7. b, 8. a, 9. c, 10. b, 11. d

Practice 2 p. 139

1. For example, Chinatown.

   Has Chinese restaurants, clothing stores, bakeries, banks, gift shops, and more.

   Because they don't need it.

   Is possible to get almost any kind of Chinese product or service in Chinatown.

   Without traveling to China.

2. Is fun to visit Los Angeles.

   If you have a car.

   Which is not fast or convenient.

   Such as the airport

   Because traffic is heavy.

   Especially in the early morning and late afternoon.

   When people are traveling to and from work.

RUN-ON SENTENCES

Practice 1 pp. 140–141

1. b, 2. b, 3. a, 4. b, 5. b, 6. a, 7. b, 8. b, 9. a, 10. b, 11. a

Practice 2 pp. 141–142

1. It's going to rain. Close the windows.
2. Hue-Ya plays the violin, and she also sings.
3. Sami fell asleep in class, and everyone laughed.
4. Let's go home. I'm tired.
5. The lake is wide, but it's not very deep.
6. A dog was barking all night, so I couldn't sleep.
7. The basketball player was huge. He was more than 7 feet tall.
8. Garlic tastes wonderful. It's also very healthy.
9. Ms. Saroyan got a job in Ankara. It is the capital of Turkey.
10. I'm so glad that movie is over. Let's go.
11. We followed the GPS, but we got lost anyway.

COMMA SPLICES

Practice 1 pp. 143–144

1. a, 2. a, 3. b, 4. a, 5. b, 6. b, 7. a, 8. b, 9. a, 10. a, 11. b

Practice 2 pp. 144–145

1. Joe is American, he works in Canada.
2. We went to our first baseball game, it was very slow.
3. I have a toothache, I need to see a dentist.
4. Baby rabbits are blind, they depend on their mothers for everything.
5. Steven finished his algebra class, then he took geometry.
6. We walked into the house, we turned on the air conditioner.
7. I stopped taking violin lessons, I never practiced.
8. There are over a hundred billionaires in the world, only a few are women.
9. The war ended, all the soldiers went home.
10. Alice turned 16, she got a job at a candy store.
11. Millions of people enjoy shopping online, it's easy and fast.

PARAGRAPH ORGANIZATION

Topic Sentence

Practice 1 p. 146

1. they are generous and hardworking.
2. Loss of habitat and hunting
3. necessary for good health.
4. the perfect place to go for your honeymoon.
5. these tips to help you lower your water bill.
6. Talent, dedication, and luck are three characteristics
7. health benefits for people of all ages.
8. the perfect place to go for a winter vacation.
9. is very hard to do and takes a lot of work.
10. For the best selection and lowest prices
11. cause people to lose both time and money.

Practice 2 pp. 147–148

1. a Journalists today need to have a number of essential skills.

2. c Alaska is a huge state with several different types of climate.

3. b Amelia Earhart lived a short but inspiring life.

4. a My physical, mental, and emotional health have improved since I stopped eating sugar.

5. c Our family vacation in Florida last month was a disaster.

Ordering

TIME ORDER

Practice 1 p. 150

To begin	then
Soon	after a while
Next	Two hours later
After that	finally
Five minutes	After 20 minutes

Practice 2 pp. 150–151

Part 1

1. fourth	3. first
2. third	4. second

Part 2

1. fourth	3. second
2. first	4. third

LISTING BY ORDER OF IMPORTANCE

Practice 1 pp. 152–153

Paragraph 1

First of all/To begin

One reason

Next/Second/In addition

Third/Next/In addition

Most of all/Most importantly/Finally

Paragraph 2

To begin/First of all

Second/Next/In addition

In addition/Third/Next

Most importantly/Most of all/Finally

Practice 2 p. 153

2. First, she is very knowledgeable.

3. She knows how to teach classes for many different ages and ability levels.

1. There are two characteristics that make my zumba teacher, Marcella, one of the best dance teachers I've ever had.

7. This makes everybody want to try harder.

5. Second, Marcella is enthusiastic.

6. While we are dancing, she constantly shouts out encouraging words to anyone who is tired or slow.

4. For example, one of the classes she teaches is called Zumba Gold, which is mainly for older people.

SPATIAL ORDERING

Practice 1 pp. 154–155

1. a, c

2. b, c

3. b, c

Practice 2 p. 156

1. b Only three states border the Pacific Ocean on the west coast of the United States.

2. a The service porch in my parent's house has several functions.

Cause and Effect
INTRODUCING CAUSES
Practice 1 pp. 157–158

Paragraph 1

We have different opinions about politics.

I want to have a big family, but Charles doesn't like children.

Charles wants to live in a big city, but I prefer to live in a small town.

Paragraph 2

The café is dirty. The chairs and tables are sticky, and the bathrooms are disgusting.

The café raised its prices recently. For example, a hamburger now costs $9, and a small salad is $4.50. That's too much.

The waiters aren't serious about their work. They talk on their cell phones instead of serving customers.

Paragraph 3

It is easy to order and return shoes.

They have a huge selection of shoes for men, women, and children.

If they don't have the shoes you want in your size, they will get them for you.

If you need help, you can always reach a friendly, helpful salesperson.

Practice 2 p. 159

Paragraph 1

People should not smoke at all because smoking has so many bad effects on people and the environment.

Paragraph 2

In addition, many people who sit and work at a computer all day may develop problems with their eyes and their weight.

INTRODUCING EFFECTS
Practice 1 p. 161

Paragraph 1

I am paying for my own rent and bills, so I am learning how to manage money.

I am learning how to cook because my mother isn't here to prepare food for me.

I can be more independent. For example, I can decide for myself when I will go out, come home, and get up in the morning.

Paragraph 2

Pets help reduce stress.

People who own pets are less lonely.

People with pets recover from illness faster.

Children who live in a home with pets have fewer allergies.

Paragraph 3.

Sports help young people develop strength and flexibility.

Playing a team sport teaches young people how to be fair and how to cooperate with others.

Young people who play sports are very busy. Therefore, they spend less time watching television and playing video games.

Practice 2 p. 162

Paragraph 1

My cousin, for example, is living with his parents, and he's using his time to develop several new software products.

Paragraph 2

In many African countries, many children only go to school for three years.

Comparison and Contrast

COMPARISON

Practice 1 p. 164

1. Mark is tall and athletic. Similarly, Jennifer is tall, and she's very good at sports.

   Both Mark and Jennifer have curly blond hair and green eyes.

   Mark has freckles, and Jennifer does, too.

   The way they walk is also very similar.

2. Their salaries are almost the same. Each of them received a starting salary of about $10.00 per hour.

   Their jobs offer similar benefits, too. Each of them receives health insurance, five days of sick leave, and two weeks of paid vacation per year.

3. Both activities are excellent forms of exercise.

   House cleaning is like gardening because both activities make my home more beautiful.

Practice 2 p. 165

1. a
2. b

CONTRAST

Practice 1 p. 167

1. The NorthAir flight is $120 cheaper than the Friend Air flight.

   NorthAir has an on-time record of 88% on flights to Boston, but Friend Air's record is only 72%.

   NorthAir planes have enough legroom for a tall person like me. In contrast, the seats on the Friend Air flight are crowded together.

   There is no checked baggage charge on NorthAir. However, Friend Air charges $35 per bag.

2. Males have bigger, heavier bones than females.

   Bones in the female body finish growing around age 18. On the other hand, bones in the male body continue to grow until age 21.

   In general, males have longer and heavier skulls than females.

   Males have longer ribs than females. Also, male ribs are more curved than female ribs.

3. African elephants have larger ears than Asian elephants.

   An African elephant can weigh up to 7,500 kilograms. In contrast, the Asian elephant typically weighs about 6,000 kilograms.

   African elephants are larger than Asian elephants. African males are about 4 meters tall; Asian males are about 3.5 meters tall.

   On an African elephant, the highest point of the body is the shoulders. On an Asian elephant, the highest point is the back.

   All African elephants have tusks, but only some male Asian elephants do.

Practice 2 p. 168

1. They do have similar ideas about energy use and preventing pollution.

2. Both sports use "rally" scoring, which means a team does not have to serve the ball to get a point.

Supporting Sentences

PROVIDING REASONS

Practice 1 p. 170

1. Amsterdam has excellent weather during the summer.
2. There are three community colleges in my town.

Practice 2 p. 171

Paragraph 1

6.

3.

1.

2.

5.

4.

Paragraph 2

2.

6.

1.

4.

5.

3.

PROVIDING DETAILS

Practice 1 pp. 172–173

1. About 4,000 people visit Antarctica each year.
2. Louis Braille is buried in the Pantheon in Paris.
3. She has an old, beat up Volkswagen Beetle.
4. I got my first credit card when I was 18 years old.
5. Some people are allergic to cats.

Practice 2 p. 174

1. One cup of broccoli contains all the vitamin C you need in a day to help you stay healthy.

   Broccoli has lots of fiber to help your digestive system work properly.

   Broccoli contains glucoraphanin, which helps the body to fight cancer.

2. In North America, greetings usually involve some form of touching—a handshake, a hug, or a kiss.

   When Thai people say hello, they press their hands together at chest level and bow their heads slightly.

   In Japan, it is traditional for people to bow when they meet and greet each other.

3. A mob can have as many as 100 kangaroos.

   The head of the mob is the largest male in the group, called a "boomer" or "old man."

   Living in a group offers protection for younger and weaker animals.

GIVING EXAMPLES

Practice 1 p. 176

My grandmother never wastes anything. For instance, she washes and reuses plastic bags.

Dorian has several interesting hobbies. For example, she goes to a belly dancing class once a week.

Honeybees communicate the location of food by dancing. A movement called the "waggle dance," for example, indicates that food is far away.

2011 was a year of amazing scientific discoveries. For instance, scientists at Oxford University developed the first vaccine against malaria.

In recent years, my city's newspaper has changed in many ways. For example, it no longer has a weekly health section.

In my city, the weather can be very unpredictable in June. For instance, the temperature can go up or down by 20 degrees in one day.

I have a special drawer where I keep my "treasures." For example, this drawer is where I keep letters from my grandfather.

Several human foods are toxic to dogs. Fruits, such as grapes and raisins, can lead to kidney failure in dogs.

My sister doesn't look like anyone else in the family. For example, she has blond hair and blue eyes, but the rest of us have dark hair and brown eyes.

Different kinds of wood are useful for different purposes. Oak, for example, is useful for making strong furniture like dining tables because it is very heavy.

Practice 2 p. 177

1. For example, she loves tomatoes.

2. For instance, she is famous as a soul singer.

3. such as the Nissan Leaf and the Chevy Volt.

4. For example, he eats leftover pizza for breakfast.

5. For instance, it can tell me the weather in any city.

6. For example, they are necessary for proper digestion.

7. An elevator, for instance, is called a lift in Britain.

8. Personal computers, for example, weighed 40 pounds at one time.

9. such as wheat, corn, and soybeans.

10. For example, loud car horns make her nervous.

11. For instance, she volunteers at a children's hospital every Saturday.

EXPRESSING OPINIONS

Practice 1 p. 179

Paragraph 1

Spanking teaches children that it is OK to hit someone if you don't like what they are doing.

Spanking is painful and cruel.

Spanking does not teach children how to correct their behavior.

Paragraph 2

According to research, art helps children develop every part of their brains.

Art helps children learn academic skills. For example, music and drawing can help students learn mathematics.

Children who are not good at traditional subjects may develop confidence by participating in art activities.

Practice 2 p. 180

Paragraph 1

2.

4.

7.

1.

6.

5.

3.

Paragraph 2

3.

9.

5.

6.

1.

8.

4.

7.

2.

The Conclusion

Practice 1   pp. 181–182

1. c To sum up, these three advantages explain why I would rather take the train to work than drive my car.

2. a In short, these reasons explain why many people would rather rent an apartment than buy a home.

3. c So enjoy your morning cup of coffee—it's good for you!

Practice 2   pp. 182–183

1. c presents the writer's opinion or final thoughts

2. a restates the topic sentence

3. b summarizes the main points

Unity

Practice 1   pp. 184–185

1. If I plant seeds, I always get excited when the first bits of green appear above the ground.

Carrying pots and bags of fertilizer keeps my muscles strong.

2. She knows how to use a computer, and enjoys writing emails to all of her family members.

She still cleans her house all by herself.

3. Don't leave water running while you brush your teeth.

Get a large container and use it to collect rainwater.

Practice 2   p. 185

1. I like watching reality shows like "Lost."

2. Today you can see fossils of ancient corn in museums.

3. You need a computer in order to take online classes.

WRITING ASSIGNMENTS

pp. 186–216

Answers will vary.

POST-TEST

Post-Test 1   pp. 234–239

1. b, 2. c, 3. c, 4. d, 5. b, 6. a, 7. b, 8. a,
9. d, 10. a, 11. a, 12. b, 13. c. 14. d, 15. b,
16. c, 17. d, 18. a, 19. d, 20. a, 21. d,
22. b, 23. a, 24. a, 25. c, 26. c, 27. b,
28. c, 29. d, 30. b, 31. b, 32. c, 33. d,
34. c, 35. d, 36. b, 37. c, 38. a, 39. b, 40. d

Post-Test 2   p. 240

Answers will vary.